A WHITE TEACHER

TEACHER
TALKS
ABOUT RACE

CLASSROOM EDITION

Julie Landsman

Rowman & Littlefield Education
Lanham • New York • Toronto • Plymouth, UK

Published in the United States of America
by Rowman & Littlefield Education
A Division of Rowman & Littlefield Publishers, Inc.
A wholly owned subsidary of The Rowman & Littlefield Publishing Group, Inc.
4501 Forbes Boulevard, Suite 200, Lanham, Maryland 20706
www.rowmaneducation.com

Estover Road
Plymouth PL6 7PY
United Kingdom

British Library Cataloguing in Publication Information Available

Library of Congress Cataloging-in-Publication Data

Landsman, Julie.
  A white teacher talks about race / Julie Landsman. — Classroom ed.
    p. cm.
  ISBN-13: 978-1-60709-064-9 (pbk. : alk. paper)
  ISBN-10: 1-60709-064-3 (pbk. : alk. paper)
  ISBN-13: 978-1-60709-065-6 (electronic)
  ISBN-10: 1-60709-065-1 (electronic)
  1. Multicultural education—United States—Case studies. 2. Minorities—Education
(Secondary)—United States—Case studies. 3. Race awareness—Study and teaching
(Secondary)—United States—Case studies. 4. Teachers, White—United States—Case
studies. 5. Landsman, Julie. I. Title.
  LC1099.3.L35 2008
  373.1829—dc22   2008046109

♾™ The paper used in this publication meets the minimum requirements of
American National Standard for Information Sciences—Permanence of Paper
for Printed Library Materials, ANSI/NISO Z39.48–1992.
Manufactured in the United States of America.

This book is dedicated to all the students I have worked with
over the twenty-five years of my career who have taught me so much about
celebration, culture, and the joy of teaching.

CONTENTS

INTRODUCTION

Our Changing World: A Cause for Celebration

*When we first came here it was against the law to practice
our rituals, to recognize our heritage. Even the drum was
forbidden. So now, when black people are just beginning to
embrace their ethnic identity, whites look at it as some sort of
threat to their hegemony. It's simply that black people are
just beginning to realize how much they've been deprived of
knowledge of their own selves.*

    *I think we must begin to realize that we are Americans of
African descent. And to be comfortable with that identity. I've
been to Africa several times, and to other countries. I know that
I am peculiarly American. There is no getting around that.*

—Salim Muwakkil, *In These Times*

I put the book down. I looked at the seventh- and eighth-graders in front
of me. I had read aloud to them a letter a man wrote to his wife in 1945,
after he and a group of Americans had liberated one of the Nazi death camps.
He told his wife that he hoped never again to see what he had seen this day,
never again to witness the evil that human beings are capable of doing to one
another. At the same time he said he wished everyone could see it; then they
might understand.

The students were unusually quiet and thoughtful. I asked them to write "I hope never again" and "I wish" at the top of their papers. They were to make one list of things they hoped would not happen again and another list of things they wished for.

They worked silently, biting on their pencils, thinking. They bent over their papers, all of them writing, absorbed. After ten minutes, I asked them to finish up. Students began to read aloud, going around in a circle. Some hoped never again to see poor people living in shelters, see old women being knocked down on the street, or hear gunfire at night. Some hoped never again to see any war; others wished their families to be reunited. Some prayed that their dog would not die, that their grandfather would get well, that their aunt from up north would keep her cabin so they could spend summers there forever. Some wished for world peace, a new Trans Am, some money for their mother so she could buy a new house.

Shantae, a black student, was the last to read: "I hope never again to feel the kind of prejudice I feel every day when I walk down the street, or go into a store, or stand in line somewhere." She had only one wish: "I wish I was an American."

Silence. Shantae's family has lived in this country since the mid-1600s. They came with the slave trade, were freed, and migrated north in the middle 1900s, centuries after their arrival on our shores in chains. Yet she does not feel American yet. No one, not any of the white, Asian, or black students in the class, questioned her last statement. They all nodded their heads in understanding.

And while I would not challenge her perception, her reality, I can hope, as any teacher would hope, that she will feel a part of this country some day. I have heard statements like Shantae's spoken by adults, by small children, and by many of the adolescents with whom I work. Yet I never get used to it. I find myself struggling with deep despair after a moment like this, wondering about the divide between white people and people of color in this country.

I believe that one of the ways that Shantae will come to feel like an American will be through seeing and hearing her ancestors' stories as part of her school experience. When we celebrate Shantae's rich culture, when we include her history, when we integrate her life into every subject in our classrooms, I believe she will begin to feel that America is a place she can truly call her country, her home. This same need for inclusion is true for Shantae's Hmong classmate and for the Somali girl who sits across from her in science.

I write this book to support all of us who work to change the way Shantae and her classmates feel, who want to encourage teachers and others in their neighborhoods, their cities, and their towns to make schools true places of inclusion. More than that, I write to celebrate the lives of students, children, young adults, men, and women, who make up the varied and rich tapestry that is the United States of America. I write for white teachers, who struggle and celebrate in classrooms across the country: to support them, to ask them to look deeply at their own stories, at the stories of the students in their rooms, and to take what they need from my story, my mistakes. For teachers of color, I write so they can read, if they want to, one white teacher's thoughts on race and education. I welcome their reactions.

I write for all of us, to help us understand ourselves, our students, and even our country.

OUR CHANGING WORLD:
WHY WE NEED TO UNDERSTAND

I teach in schools where at least 60 to 80 percent of my students are not of European-American descent. More and more, our public schools are dominated by students who are black, Asian, Latino/a, Native American, and new immigrants. I teach students who have been in the United States for many generations and students who have arrived only months ago. Many of my students do not speak English as their first language.

In our twenty-five largest cities, students of color are in the majority in all but two. By some estimates, 40 percent of our students will be of color in all classrooms in the United States by the year 2000.

Many people feel that these numbers are alarming. I find them a cause for celebration. I believe we have much more to gain than to lose by these changes. I am confident that the diversity of cultures in our buildings, the mixture of clothing, dialects, and music in the hallways, can only increase our knowledge, our joy, and our excitement and can only add to the quality of our lives. I also believe that the presence of more students of color will increase the standards for our students in reading, writing, math, and science, as well as in compassion, cooperation, and global knowledge.

OUR CHANGING WORLD: A CONCERN

At the same time, I am concerned that even as the percentage of students of color is increasing, the percentage of teachers of color is shrinking. They make up only 10 percent of the teachers in public schools now and even that percentage is diminishing. When I walk down the hallways of high schools in and around the city and see mostly white adults in the principals' offices and in front of the classrooms, I feel disheartened. I want to see more teachers who are African American, Asian American, Latino/a American, or Native American. I used to believe this was important primarily in integrated schools of the cities. Now I am convinced we need men and women of color who love kids in our schools in the suburbs, teaching in primarily white schools as well.

WHITE TEACHERS CAN
PROVIDE INCLUSIVE CLASSROOMS

While we wait for the demographics of the teaching profession to catch up to the demographics of the classroom, I am confident we white teachers are up to the job of working in these mixed environments. I know there is a history of benign racism among white teachers in all-black classrooms, but I believe this can change.

Over the years, I have observed many of my white colleagues creating classrooms that are vibrant, exciting places to be; and these are classrooms where the majority of students are of color. The best of these classrooms inspire and challenge all students because they are places where students can bring their lives, their concerns, and their abilities right into school. I have been privileged to be part of teams with gifted and devoted educators who believe in the potential of every young man and woman in their classroom.

There is still nothing like the high I feel at the end of a good teaching day. Much of the reason for my exhilaration has to do with the interplay of cultures, voices, humor, and effort that I see before me. As I head into retirement, I am convinced I will not experience exactly this kind of satisfaction and joy again.

Although white teachers can teach students of color effectively, they need support. Like all teachers, they need parents and businessmen and-women, workers in community agencies and those in the legal and medical fields to become involved in the classroom, to push for small class sizes for all public school students, and to advocate for decent technology and working conditions for everyone.

All of us dealing with issues of race and culture in America today, be we teachers or day-care providers, lawyers or corporate executives, mechanics or computer programmers, need to be honest: honest about ourselves and what we carry with us into our places of work. I am finally getting to the point where I can listen without defensiveness or guilt when friends or students of color point out my mistakes, question my understanding of their experience, or describe something I did as offensive. It is never going to be easy. Yet I believe it is the most important thing I can do.

WILLING TO TALK

In colleges and high schools today, most white teachers are hesitant to bring up what stares at us with brown or blue eyes, what is so obvious when we see a coffee-colored, freckled, or dark blue-black hand resting on a white page. We believe we are "colorblind," a notion from the '50s, and from the Reagan years when it was considered wrong to recognize our differences. We white people hide from the fact of skin color difference. We often fail to speak directly at work about students who are different from ourselves. We do speak about it, though. After work, at dinner tables, we use euphemisms, code words: "welfare problem," "poverty problem," "crime problem," assuming these mean something other than what they are—a back-handed way of talking about what we believe is a "race problem."

Teachers are not alone in such hesitation. Many of us, in many walks of life, are nervous talking about race. We are so often afraid we will say the wrong thing, and so we say nothing. We become quiet, defensive, ashamed, or unwilling to respond. We pretend that racial differences do not exist; we are all alike under the skin, aren't we? Thus, we do not acknowledge the experiences of people of color, precisely *because* of their skin—black, brown, yellow, or white, dark or light.

In schools, or even at our dinner tables, at the very same time adults avoid it, students and young people want to talk about race. Yet if it comes up, we move to something else, quickly, furtively, nervous about what might happen if we really allow our students, or our own sons and daughters, to get into it. And so we refuse to provide a place where students like Tyrone, an African-American young man who attends the school where I teach, can come and talk about the racial situation for him at his job in a suburban neighborhood. We avoid a discussion of how this same job might be different for him than it is for his white friend Kent. We fail to respond to Sheila when she describes trying to get a cab to take her and her baby to the hospital emergency room: how ten cabs will go by her to stop for a white woman just up the block before one will stop for them.

For those of us who are white, I believe avoidance comes because we are afraid of our own racism. At the same time, we want to remain comfortable with our interpretations of issues around race, even if they are inaccurate or just plain wrong. I notice that at the same time that we talk about the increase of teen mothers in the black community, we refuse to see the white faces of those on welfare. We pass by the pale bodies of those who serve us at fast food restaurants; ignore the unhealthy look to the skin of a thin white woman who steals tuna for the children who ride listlessly in her shopping cart. We are uncomfortable when we learn that criminals are white men as well as men of color, when white children bring guns to school and shoot teachers or classmates; when we are confronted with the face of evil that is as pale as our son's or daughter's light skin. We speak about how black students all eat at the same lunch table, ignoring the tables made up of all white students.

We who are white do not want to talk about our white skin or explore what "whiteness" has to do with all that is going on in our own lives and in the lives of our students. Now, I believe, more than ever, it is time to talk. It is time to let our children talk and our colleagues talk.

It is time to study our memories: to explore what it was in our childhood that formed our racial definitions, our prejudices. It is time to let our students teach us, to look for historians who will tell us the whole truth, to look for activists who can inform us. It is time to make mistakes and learn from them.

As I write this book I am celebrating my twenty-fifth year of teaching, most of it in city public schools. Many of those years have been spent working with students in serious trouble: truants, disruptive students, or those who were sent to special programs by the courts because they were involved in criminal activity.

Seven years ago I took a leave from Minneapolis to teach at the new State Arts High School. I did this to take a break from the intensity of working with young men and women in constant trouble and crisis, and as a chance to teach creative writing. This school was 89 percent white. While I liked my students, and while I found they were experiencing a surprising amount of despair and cynicism, after three years I became uncomfortable in such a homogeneous environment. I missed the accents, the mixed-up voices and songs in the hallways. I missed city kids. I wanted to be part of it again: the languages, the cultures, the dress, and the music in the hallways.

So I returned to Minneapolis, to a school on a rundown part of River Street, to a classroom across from a used car lot. This is the kind of school I write about in this book—a day at the Academic Support Program, or ASP. I have changed the name of the school in order to preserve the privacy of the students and teachers there. I have also changed the names of teachers, counselors, and students. The individuals are based on real students, with some personal and situational details altered. I believe that naming the school would focus on a single building—its strengths and weaknesses—instead of on the broader issues that I hope readers will think about when reading about this day. The problems in this school are similar to problems in many schools, both regular and alternative, all over the country.

ASP is a school for students who have complicated lives. Some are overwhelmed trying to parent their own children. Others want to leave the gang they have been a part of for three years. A small percentage of them are trying to survive by living as squatters in condemned buildings. Some of the students have dealt or are dealing drugs. Some are runaways. A number of students are from well-off families. These young people have become so bored or turned off, they have stopped attending their home high school. Yet while some of the students at ASP are white and some are middle class, the majority are working class and/or poor. Most of them are black, Hmong, Native American, Latino/a, and Vietnamese. These young men and women have come to this alternative school *not* because they are unintelligent or unable to do school work. Many of them are extremely bright. They have come to school because they want to complete high school and need an individualized approach to the requirements.

And so, in returning to ASP, I returned to young people who are brilliant, demanding, and funny.

THIS BOOK

In this book I depict a composite day of teaching, which includes my visit to a mainstream middle school as a writer. I also describe the education class I teach at a local university. I wanted to construct a book that allowed for reflections on race while at the same time portraying students, actual dialogue, and incidents that occurred in my teaching life.

I begin with reflections before school, to show the reader some of what I bring into the classroom before the first bell even rings.

During the day I describe some fine young people: Tyrone, Sheila, Leah, Josh, Sara, and Ka. I cannot tell you what they are thinking, but I can tell you what they say, show you their honesty, their observations, and their solutions. I believe it is among the students who are African American, Asian American, Latino/a, and Native American—not only those who are white—that we will find important role models to lead us into a new time. In our city classrooms are students who are willing to have the important dialogues, interactions, disputes, and differences with each other that allow them to understand other cultures. It is these students who have learned to get along—without fanfare, without national attention, without any credit for what they accomplish each day. They are on the front lines, working with each other, agreeing, disagreeing, making mistakes, living their lives in the multicultural society that America is becoming. I am not saying that there are no racist white students at ASP or that all of the African-American students are eager to get along with whites. There are racists at ASP, as in any school. I am saying, however, that those white students and students of color who sincerely try to find their place in these diverse classrooms are individuals we need to watch and, perhaps, to emulate.

Race and racism are complicated subjects. They are multifaceted: a prism turned perpetually in different directions, light breaking at a multitude of angles, revelations. Poverty, culture, and ethnicity are all part of this prism, this complexity of light. Many days I have wanted to give up on writing this book.

Yet not to write or speak openly about race is evasion. To decide, as I have been tempted to do, that "everyone is an individual and so we cannot even talk of the effects of race" is a cop-out. It is the trick that whites in the United States have used for decades: the rugged individualist, the Horatio Alger myth, the escape clause in our contract with humanity.

I have one major concern, and it is this: because my work with students on this day is primarily with those students who have problems in school and who have attended the alternative high school depicted here, I may be reinforcing a stereotype. I may be adding to the portrayal of students of color as being unsuccessful or unwilling to participate in mainstream culture. I hope that my readers will immediately see that one of the things I want to do is to deconstruct such stereotypes by presenting these alternative students, some of them involved in gangs, in all their complexity and intelligence. I am a firm believer that students at any age can become successful. My most hopeful experiences have been with just those students who have been labeled failures.

After my first book, *Basic Needs: A Year with Street Kids in a City School,* was published, my father, with whom I have never agreed about much of anything, said to me: "I gotta admit, Julie. After reading your book, I can't look at those punk kids on the corner quite the same any more."

I can only hope this book will have a similar effect. I have also taught in mainstream high schools, middle schools, and even elementary schools in suburbia and the city. I reflect on my experiences in all these settings during the course of *A White Teacher Talks about Race.* I believe my story will resonate with not only teachers but with those who are thinking about how they live out their racial memories.

A NOTE TO THE READER
ABOUT LANGUAGE

This book raises serious issues about teaching, culture, race, and privilege. The central terms of the title, and of the book, *white* and *race,* are a problem. *Race* is a word, a concept that is full of ambiguity. Old cultures, Western and non-Western—Greece and China, for example—have always distinguished between themselves and outsiders. It is a universal phenomenon. But the term *race,* as used in the nineteenth and twentieth centuries, is more than that. It is part skin color, part privilege, and part social construction. White people do not usually think of themselves as having a race; race is a marker for "the other." When we refer to a person, without further description, the social norm is white (and male and straight and not disabled). We typically refer to the "black lawyer" or the "woman doctor." The assumptions embedded in the language enshrine whiteness and white privilege. If you are white, you need no further description. In this book, I have struggled to use the term *race* and refer to race in a consistent way. I know I have not succeeded; I know that it is impossible to fully succeed.

In his book *How the Irish Became White,* Noel Ignatiev explores the issues of how race, and particularly "whiteness," are socially defined and socially constructed. I think that this book, among many others, can give you a start on grappling with the theoretical issues that have gone into my thinking about these themes. The book before you is not a book of theory; it is one person's attempt to come to grips with the reality of race at a particular time and in a particular place. Others have done the theorizing. This is about my life and the lives of my students.

TERMINOLOGY

> *The original creation of racial categories was in the service of oppression. Some may argue that to continue to use them is to continue that oppression. I respect that argument. Yet it is difficult to talk about what is essentially a flawed and problematic social construct without using language that is itself problematic. We have to be able to talk about it in order to change it. So this is the language I choose.*
>
> —Beverly Tatum,
> *Why Are All the Black Kids Sitting Together in the Cafeteria?*

The previous paragraph sums up my feelings about terminology used in this book. I have done the best I can and know I have not done a perfect job of selecting what words to use. There have been days, as I have struggled with writing about race, when I have wondered whether I should even try to capture my thoughts. Being brought up a good white Anglo-Saxon Protestant in the '50s, I was constantly afraid I would offend someone. Thus, I am aware that the following terms may not work for all readers. They are my compromise, my solution, in order to feel free to speak about this at all. I believe they are better than continuing to remain silent.

I refer to *African American* and *black* throughout the text. African American is used in reference to culture, black to skin color.

I use the terms *Latino/a, Asian American,* and *Native American* to talk about persons who identify with these groups.

I use the terms *white* and *European American* in relationship to skin color and culture, respectively.

I have used the terms *students of color* and *people of color* to describe those peoples in the United States who have been historically oppressed by racism.

I am aware of the simplistic nature of such references and only hope the reader will bear with this linguistic solution for a situation that language cannot address adequately.

BEFORE SCHOOL

What I Bring

Wherever the Negro face appears a tension is created, the tension of a silence filled with things unutterable. It is a sentimental error, therefore, to believe that the past is dead; it means nothing to say that it is all forgotten, that the Negro himself has forgotten it. It is not a question of memory. Oedipus did not remember the thongs that bound his feet; nevertheless the marks they left testified to that doom toward which his feet were leading him. The man does not remember the hand that struck him, the darkness that frightened him, as a child; nevertheless, the hand and the darkness remain with him, indivisible from himself forever, part of the passion that drives him wherever he thinks to take flight.

—James Baldwin, *Many Thousands Gone*

MY SKIN

Before the weather heats up, and before I get ready to go to school, Max, my Sheltie, and I head for our morning walk along the Mississippi River. We are walking between Minneapolis and St. Paul, Minnesota, across two bridges that join the cities, cities that sit solidly on this river, in the center of the North Central United States. While our northern border separates us from Canada, we will not feel any of that cool Canadian air today. It is May, and there is a predicted high of 88 degrees.

I move past two men on a bench who are passing a flask back and forth. I cross the Lake Street Bridge, look down at the flat water below me. This river is the same one that runs through the city where my father grew up, East St. Louis, Illinois. His name was Boone Tarleton Guyton. He was white. My name before I married was Julie Guyton.

One Monday morning, years ago, Mae Gossett, an older black woman, came in to the school where we worked. She told me she had just met a family of Guytons from Missouri at her church the day before.

"Girl, I do believe you are related to black folk," Mae chuckled. She reached her arm around me and pulled me close. I liked what she said. I wanted to believe her. Yet, of course, despite what Mae Gossett had said, despite the black Guytons from Missouri who are in the world, or the black writers, musicians, poets, and basketball players who are named Guyton, I know I am not black. I am white. My skin is white, and, more important, I have been treated all my life as a white person. So, as much as I would like to lean back against Mae's shoulder and blend in with her gentle teasing, become black for a few minutes, I know that is impossible.

MY CULTURE

My background is: East St. Louis jazz clubs, Southern cooking, and the work ethic from my father's side; New England Puritanism, pot roast, and classical music on my mother's side. This is my mixture of cultures. Both of my parents, despite their different cultures, were white.

My Jewish husband, Maury, comes from latkes, Yiddish, brisket, and dancing the hora at weddings: his culture. So while both of us are white, our cultures are different.

Greta, a young Ukrainian immigrant in a writing class I teach across the city, comes from a certain kind of cooking, language, music, and custom. She is white and will be treated differently in this country from Mai, her Hmong classmate, even though both young women arrived in this country about the same time. She will be treated differently not so much because of her culture but because of the white color of her skin.

same race different nationalities?

Sarah, another white student of mine, is a street kid, often living in squatter's apartments in condemned buildings near the school. Yet when she and Sheila, who is black, accompany me into a bookstore, Sheila will be followed and watched closely, while Sarah will wander without such surveillance.

MY FEARS

At this moment, I can see two white men who have come to stand under the railroad trestle. They are partially hidden in the shadows under the bridge, but I can see that they hold bright aluminum cans of beer in their large hands. I go quickly past them. The dog is already panting, the cicadas beginning their insistent whine, 5:30 A.M. I can hear, over these sounds, voices of more men down the steep bank, all the way to the river itself. Sounds of a party, too early.

The humidity brings the smell of asphalt and river sludge, of cut grass and wet dog, and it surrounds me. The barges move like flat landing carriers in the middle of the water. An old Asian man and woman fish along the opposite bank the way they have for years. Men lie on the gay beach across the water. They still have white winter bodies that I can see whenever they stand upright to wave at the slim boats of rowers that go by. The coxswain counts the beat and the women's arms, the men's arms are in perfect syncopation on the varsity crew boats.

I am afraid of finding myself down there. My fear is not of the Asian couple or the gay men. It is not of the black men who stand with patience at dawn, fishing. No. I am afraid I will be down there at the white boys' party, the one I hear from up above. I am afraid of being surrounded by men, the only woman: being "the only."

The only

The students at ASP have told me about similar fears, fears of being "the only." Sheila does not like to be the only black student at any gathering and avoids this at all costs. Preston will not go into a restaurant if there are no black people sitting there. Tyrone does not ever want to live in a white suburb because of the way he has been treated there when he delivers mail. Sarah does not seem to be afraid of being anywhere, and Leah rarely leaves her neighborhood.

And so, they bring to my room each day their own fears, their experiences of being "the only" in a hostile environment. And while I know there are similarities in our fears, in our histories, in our bodies, and in how we register such fears, I also know I come with a set of *white woman* fears. They come with *black man* fears, *black woman* or *poor woman* histories. In one single place we come to talk each day.

set of fears (handwritten)

MY WORDS

As I reach the other side of the river and look back across to the beach where the men are popping cans already empty, I pass a black woman who runs each day with two large German shepherds. The woman and I smile at each other.

A few minutes later I hear talking behind the trees as two people approach me.

"Nigger, you better be careful with that mouth or you gonna be in serious trouble, man. I mean she gonna whip your ass talkin' like that!" Laughter.

Two black men jog past me. The word *nigger* hangs in the air after they go. I cannot get used to it, not even when I have heard it among black students in the hallways for years, not even when I hear it in hip hop lyrics. I bristle at it, no matter who it comes from.

I learned what that word meant when I was four:

It is 1948 in Texas. I am playing eeny meeny miney mo with my sister, Lesley, two years old. We are deciding who gets the last cookie. We are sitting in the kitchen of my parents' large home in a suburb just outside of Dallas. It is hot, even inside. It is always hot, or rainy and mud thick, in this new housing development. A black woman, Lillian, who cleans our house, is at the counter, fixing food for my baby brother.

I say, "Eeny meeny miney mo, catch a nigger by his toe." →shocked! (handwritten)

My father taught this rhyme to me in my early years.

When I say *nigger*, Lillian walks over to where we are and sits down, across from me. She pulls me forward, holding my hands so I am standing in front of her, looking into her eyes. She is quite thin. Her face has high cheekbones. She wears a pale blue dress and a scarf to cover her head. She says, "It would be good if you did not use that word, *nigger*. It hurts my feelings."

That day, I looked at her and I promised I would not say it ever again, I was sorry. She touched me gently on my knee, got up slowly, and went back to the sink. I grabbed the cookie and jumped down off the table, then went out onto the porch.

And even now, as I stand here, quiet for a moment before the view of the long, winding river, I can feel my body stopped there in that kitchen. I can feel the new sensation of coldness that ran through my arms and legs. I can still smell the dusty wind that blew on me out on that porch, still hear the sound of Lillian back at the sink, emptying a pan, running water over the baby bottles that waited to be cleaned.

This was a time when my body registered pain all through the pathways to my heart. It felt worse than anything I had felt before, to be told that I hurt someone.

I believe now that it is in these moments—in the education we receive that has nothing to do with school—that we are formed. In the heat of our kitchens, in the back of a car, in the check-out lines in stores: this is where our learning takes place. Here is where our impulses are born, our instincts created. And we bring all this into our classrooms, boardrooms, and meeting places.

MY NAME

Max and I cross the Franklin Avenue Bridge and begin the last quarter of our walk, again along the river. His pace slows a little. I tug at his leash. We pass the trestle and head back off River Road, home. When we get to the kitchen, Max spins around after I unleash him and he will not stop spinning until I give him a biscuit. My husband, Maury, is upstairs taking a shower. I fix coffee, putter around the table, glance at the stove. I must clean this house. It is one of those things I put off, like the garden I am always intending to put in.

In Woodbridge, Connecticut, surrounded by the roses my father loved to plant, I lived in a house cleaned by a black woman named Anne Williams. All during my childhood, in Dallas or Connecticut, the hands that cleaned the rooms where I grew up were black. The arms that lifted laundry up and pinned it to the line outside in the yard were dark next to pale sleeves. And for years I called black women old enough to be my grandmother by their first names: Anne, Marcia, Sara, Lillian. I was taught to do this, as I was taught to call my mother's friends: Mrs. Stoddard, Mrs. Ahlfeld, Mrs. Gilbert.

The students in my classes have never been able to call me Julie, even though I tell them it is all right. They insist on Mrs. Landsman or just Landsman. I have found, over the years, that I like this, I feel comfortable with it. They also insist I learn their names exactly, will stop if I mispronounce a name or spell it wrong. My day revolves around naming; learning new names,

Note

5

invented names. On average, six new students come into my classroom every other week when I am at the Academic Support Program. Their names are not easy for me: Shylala, Ma, Kai, Donieka, Chitra, Pavroom, Tameka.

My hearing has gotten slightly worse as I have gotten older, and I have to ask to have names repeated. My students show an unusual amount of tension around this request, an impatience that seems disproportionate. Even the more quiet students insist that I pronounce their names correctly. Naming is not a casual thing for these young men and women. They bring their own histories of naming, being named. Some of it goes back to slave names, their own taken from their forefathers or foremothers or given by white traders. Some of the students in my classes are tired of having to repeat their names for people; they want us to get it right immediately. Some have been through important naming ceremonies in camps in Thailand. Their names are crucial to their identity.

Until I worked with these young men and women, I took names casually. I was trained in this. Now I try to unlearn such nonchalance. I struggle with unfamiliar sounds, match the names to the faces as quickly as possible.

MY PAST

Our bedroom, where I get out of my running clothes, is the one elegant room in my house. It has steps that lead down into a large open space with windows on all sides and a fireplace at one end. Our bed is set back into an alcove. I love this room because it feels like it rests in the trees. It reminds me of past rooms, places I have lived.

I am from a kind of "out East" elegance, from St. Margaret's boarding school elegance, where there was almost no one in my life who was not white, Protestant, and wealthy. When the first Jewish girl was admitted to this school, the administrators assigned her the only single room: a converted maid's room that had never been used before she arrived. Years later they gave this same room to the only black student. This is the place where I spent my adolescence.

MY BODY

I step into the shower and feel the water on my bare skin. I remember Washington, D.C., where I went to college in the middle '60s. I had chosen to leave an exclusive woman's college to go to school in D.C. because I was interested in politics. For me, those later college years were a heady time of civil rights work, marches to Montgomery, Alabama, with Martin Luther King, and anti–Vietnam War demonstrations. These were years of activism, hope, and a faith that we could change things for the better. In the last of those years a black man raped me in the middle of one long afternoon. My body remembers this, too.

The morning following the rape the cops came to take me to an arraignment, hoping I would spot the man who had raped me the day before. They put me in the back seat of the squad car, where I sat, alone. I noticed the back of their pink necks, fringed with white hair. I watched as they smoked cigarettes and balanced cups of coffee between their legs as they ate fried egg sandwiches, never once turning around.

Later, when I said that the man they told me to watch at the arraignment was not the man who raped me but, rather, was too thin and had a different bone structure to his face, they were disappointed. They asked me if I was sure about this. I told them that the man they told me to finger was too short and did not have a roll of fat around his belly, unlike the man with whom I had spent two hours the afternoon before. The policemen shrugged and then bent close to my face, with egg still on their breath. One of them said, in a whisper, that if I wanted to, I could still finger this guy anyway, that "getting one of them niggers was just as good as getting another." → *Dr. Salaam*

The other cop nodded his head, agreeing with his partner.

I was so afraid that day, of the cops and of the man who still roamed the streets. Later I became even more afraid, to go out alone on the streets, to be alone in the apartment I had moved to immediately after being raped. I believe we take such fear in and that it has a smell. I gave it off for years. Those cops smelled of it, too. Coming from them, it had a Southern scent, all mixed in with Alabama and Mississippi speech: a rich odor of resentment and anger.

I bring this body, with both these memories, into my classroom each day. And so do my students bring theirs. We encompass all the sorrowful stories from our lives: my silence after I was raped and my scar, the small one on my right hand where he cut me as a warning, as a way of silencing me. Tyrone's body remembers being thrown up against a car, stopped for no reason; Leah lives with the memory of her mother being followed in a department store the week before Christmas. A gesture, a tone of voice, a casualness about learning a name, the way a white person turns aside when a black student wants to talk or has his

everybody goes through something.

hand up: all these accumulate in the lives of the students who enter my room. It is all we can do to find common ground.

I struggle with pronunciation, memory. They struggle with what they want to be called, what they will call me. We name things constantly for each other.

Later, showered and dressed, I drive to work. As I pull into the parking lot, grab my briefcase, and walk into the building, Leah waves from the doorway where she stands, smoking.

There are kids wandering in the halls, waiting at doors, slumped against the walls. Sheila is waiting, and so is a new student, his schedule change in his hand. I look at their bodies, try to understand what they are saying by the way they lean, smile, or frown. I fumble with my key, open the door to my room, and start this day.

REFLECTION QUESTIONS

1. How was race and its implications explained to you as a child? Did your family spend time talking about race or culture? Do you do this with your own children?
2. What are your fears around the issue of race and racism? How might this affect your teaching? Your interaction with your colleagues? Do you think this affects people of your race the same as those of other cultures or races?
3. What should teachers do about the use of the N-word? In literature classes when it shows up in books students are reading? When white students use it toward students of color? When black students use it while singing lyrics or talking with each other?
4. How do you think your whiteness influences your teaching if you are white? How does being black or Latino, Asian or Native American influence your teaching?

2

WAITING FOR
FIRST HOUR

"I got to choose between a phone and food," Sheila says while she shifts her one-year-old, Ayana, onto her other hip. She has followed me into the classroom and stands across from my desk as I put away my purse.

Sheila, who suffers from asthma, has difficulty breathing the already humid air. She gets out her inhaler and puts it up to her nose. Her hair is pulled back in a ponytail. Her Bulls jacket hangs off her thin shoulders. Some days Sheila looks like a model, her hair in tiny beaded dreads, her clothes tight-fitting and elegant. Today, though, she simply looks tired, a little disheveled. Her light brown skin is tinged slightly gray.

Seeing her upset, I remember that yesterday I asked Sheila to make a list of her fears. She wrote:

1. I'm afraid I have to go to too many more funerals.
2. I'm afraid of sounds at night when the wind blows.
3. I'm afraid I will get fat.
4. I'm afraid my brother Leon get killed. So many black boys getting killed.
5. I'm afraid of dogs when they loose and running in a group.
6. I'm afraid of getting hurt when I love somebody too much.
7. I'm afraid of Ayana, my baby, getting raped.
8. I'm afraid my Ayana gonna grow up and get in a fight with her boyfriend and then wanna come back on home and live with me.

So sad but true

Today, Sheila is simply trying to make a decision between two things that are crucial to her.

"I need to be able to call when I get sick with the asthma." She says this as she pulls up a chair across from where I sit. While she talks, I try to arrange attendance cards, read over the school bulletin, get ready for the day.

"But Ayana needs more food these days. I don't got enough money for both."

I look at her. She is seventeen years old and worried about her baby. She is a good mother. I know this. I have seen her holding Ayana, pointing out the window, showing her the buildings, the cars, the different-colored flags on the used car lot across the street. She shows me children's books from the library, laughs about how they both fall asleep over *Good Night Moon*. She gives this child more attention than some of the women I know who work at high-powered jobs, than some of the men I meet at parties, who leave their families for weeks at a time to travel. I cannot understand a country, a society that does not provide her, a child herself, with all she needs to make it, to feel safe and healthy.

"Maybe you could get one of those special vouchers from welfare. They might allow you to get a phone and keep your check the same."

"Maybe." She looks doubtful.

"Why don't you call your caseworker? You can use my phone."

Ayana is smiling at me now, finally relaxed against her mother. Sheila reaches up to the shelf and brings the phone down next to her. She dials the number. I get up for a moment and arrange some disks in holders, where students will pick them up before heading over to a computer to work on their writing. My class is one for English credit in creative writing. It is individualized so that each student can come in and work on his or her own.

"When you think she will be in?" Sheila is asking the receptionist at the welfare office. She waits, tugging at the curled extension cord. "Okay then, I'll call back later." She hangs up the phone and leans back in her chair.

"I don't know what I'm gonna do. And my rent be going up soon, I know it." Sheila lives in an efficiency apartment in a part of the city that is becoming "renovated."

"Let's try and get to one thing at a time," I tell her, as I look through an essay a student has slipped under my door.

Hard decision

easy to lose sight of dreams w/ challenges

"Yeah." Sheila catches my eye and smiles. I smile back.

Sheila has told me she does not want to have any more kids until she is finished with a two-year college or even a four-year one. She has great plans for a future in computers. She loses sight of these plans when her asthma returns full force. Hearing her pull in air and the harshness of her breathing, I am suddenly frightened for her and Ayana and all the young women all around me who cannot get help. She gets some support from her mother, but Mrs. Parker works two jobs as it is.

I turn to her. "Have you begun writing your—"

All of a sudden, Leah bursts in.

"I'ma get the bitch Leticia that was talkin' to my boyfren' last night," she yells. "I know the bitch is trying to move in on Ramon." Leah's sweatshirt is soiled, her hair sticking out from her head. She is a dark-skinned girl with large eyes that move around the room the whole time she is talking.

Her voice comes at me at full volume. " I'ma get that girl with her sorry skinny ass self, I catch her near Ramon again, with her smile all up in his face. I'ma get her sorry ass."

Sheila says, "Shhh, now, girl. The whole *school* gonna hear your business."

Leah responds, "I don't care, girl! They can know *all* my business if they want."

Sheila says nothing more. She knows Leah is connected to the Vice Lords Gang and she becomes cautious. Sheila spends much of her life keeping herself out of situations where she will run into conflict, rivalry, or disputes over territory.

Before I can say anything, Leah leaves, looking for Leticia. She still sounds angry, muttering. I know from working with her all year that Leah is often afraid. Yet she rarely talks about her fears; she covers her feelings with bravado, intimidation.

Sheila sits back down, shakes her head. She says, "Now that girl, she crazy. She gonna get herself in some serious mess!" She breathes into her inhaler. Her daughter becomes restless on her lap.

Right now, waiting for students to come into class, I hear a lot of this false bravado or breathless anxiety in the muffled conversations outside my door. I am aware every day of the guns that bring the students down: the specifics of homicide rates among young black men; the interweaving of poverty, street life,

note this

and the proliferation of weapons in all of our lives. It is no mere coincidence that this program, for students who have been failed by our system, is 80 percent black, combined with others who are Latino/a and Asian. About 10 percent of my students are white. Here, in these halls, is the intersection of race, poverty, and culture. Here, our failure as a country, as a system, to meet the needs of people of color is blatant, transparent.

[handwritten margin note: country failing these students]

For now, I plan exercises, find books that students might want to read, look up phone numbers of social service agencies, scour the want ads in the paper, create a form for revising a five-paragraph essay for college applications. There are many days when what I do seems so insignificant. There are many days when I want to run for office, work to become president, find a way to change things on a larger level than in this room, with these papers in front of me, the necessity to help Sheila find a scholarship. Yet then I would not be with the kids, be able to watch their eyes light up, listen to their jokes. So I stay in the small universe of the school and I hope for change to come.

[handwritten margin note: point of being a teacher]

Ten minutes before first hour officially begins, I send Sheila and Ayana to the social worker. After this, Sheila will drop Ayana off at the day-care center downstairs. I sit down, look through folders, and wait for more students to wander in.

UNDERSTANDING

[handwritten note: To know vs understand]

There are certain things that I, a white person, cannot *know*. According to my American Heritage Dictionary, to *know* is to "understand as fact or truth, to apprehend clearly and with certainty; to have established or fixed in mind or memory." My memories are white. I cannot *know* what it is like to·be any other color than my own white color. I cannot *know* what it is like to be poor.

[handwritten margin note: Important]

To *understand* is defined as: "to perceive the meaning of, grasp the idea of, comprehend, to be thoroughly familiar with, apprehend clearly the character, nature, or subtleties of, to be conversant." I am convinced that if I can *imagine,* I might be able to *understand.*

If I can think like a novelist, I might be able to perceive meanings, grasp ideas, and truly comprehend what others say. I was raised to believe I will always stay warm, yet I might try and place myself in the mind of the poor white character in a story who is cold. I can try to imagine the cold in the window of a winter apartment in St. Paul, no heat because the gas bill hasn't been paid in three months. I must imagine then: curling into a corner for protection from the cold one morning when there is no sound from the furnace, no rumbling and complaining belch before it pumps something basic, warmth.

I was raised to believe I will always eat. I cannot say I know what it is like to be afraid I will not eat. To understand hungry students, then, what I have to imagine is wanting for food.

I am someone who was raised to believe I should be welcomed wherever I go. If I am a reader of fiction, I might try to *imagine* the character, a young black woman, being followed around each store she enters, living in the suburbs, trying to find clothes for her children before school starts.

I believe we are all entitled to the things I have: food, warmth, a house, a way to get from home to work and back again, a safe place for my child to grow, the freedom to wander through stores without being followed or harassed. Because I have had these basic necessities, I have to continually imagine what it is like not to have such things.

Now, Sheila comes back from the social worker, sits down, breathes in, breathes out with difficulty. Watching her, listening to her, I want us all to become novelists. I want us all to listen and observe, withhold judgment as someone tells us her story. I want us to find a way in

A short time later, Leah returns. She sits down hard.

"What happened?" I ask.

"You know, same ol' same ol'. I jus' wanna get that bitch. I went lookin' for her, but she's no where today. She's 'sposed to be in Johnson's class but she's not there."

Leah is still breathing hard. She sounds as though she has been running.

Sheila withdraws to a place at the back of the room. She is still listening to Leah's story.

"Man, I just wanna get her. And Ramon, too, he be talkin' all kinds of shit to Leticia, be smilin'." Leah's hands are in fists. She slumps in her seat.

Sheila yells, "Just forget it all girl; forget the he-say, she-say, and go on with your business."

Leah does not look like she is sure she wants to do this.

"I know where her crib is, man. I know where she live at, over on the southside. I be knowin' her man, too."

Sheila shrugs her shoulders and leans back on the sagging blue couch at the other end of the room.

Leah shrugs her shoulders, too. I hand her her folder and her disk. She looks at me for a moment. Yesterday she refused to work at all. She takes the disk and puts it into the computer in front of her. Today, then, she has decided to work.

I glance at my watch and see that there are a few minutes left before first hour. Sheila has fallen asleep on the couch. Her breathing is still labored. Leah frowns in concentration, trying to decide what to add to her autobiography.

Now, Tyrone Lewis comes in to sit and read the paper in my room before his day starts. He is a stocky young man with red-brown skin. He has a small mustache, large brown eyes, and short hair cut close in a careful fade. His pants are neatly pressed, his shirt collar crisp and clean against his skin. Even in this heat he wears a sweatshirt. He is drowsy and pulls the hood up over his head. This is his signal to me that he does not want to talk right now.

Three months ago he found Nathan McCall's book *Makes Me Wanna Holler* in the media center. For awhile, he stopped by my room before heading to his job at the post office. He read aloud to me whole paragraphs that astounded him because of the accurate way they related to his own life. He also wrote a response to the book. This is a paraphrase of that response:

> This is reality. There are no referees to call a foul for me when I have been treated unfairly. I once considered this life to be a game. I have seen people spend their entire lives the whole time trying to make a better life and sometimes, just survive. In the end they die and it seems as if they did not accomplish anything. In this world death can be no harder than a life in poverty.
>
> Nathan McCall was one of the many who overcame the walls. There is no way around them, no way to climb them, no way to go under. The only way out is to go through. Once an opening is found, no alarms go off, others are not alerted to a way of escape, so only a few get away before the wall is mended. Then we all wait until someone else is strong enough to make another break through the invisible barrier.

[handwritten margin note: invisible barrier / No avoidance]

This is the same Tyrone who, when asked to write about a fantasy vacation, instead of writing about California, Florida, cruises, or warm beaches, as most of the students did, wrote in great detail about wanting a day on his block free of violence. He described this imaginary day: kids could play out on the front steps, women could sit and talk, men could bend over the open hoods of cars together, right there in the street, in the middle of a summer afternoon.

For the past few weeks Tyrone has been trying to get his own brother, Johnny, to leave the apartment that he, Ty, has finally rented in a "good" section of town. Johnny is dealing drugs. Ty himself has done his time in prison, has been in a gang. He writes about breaking and entering homes, stealing jewelry and stereos. But now he wants to keep his good job at the post office, finish high school, and go on. Tyrone has said all year that he wants to stay out of his former gang life, once and for all.

He slumps in the chair, drums his fingers on the desk. Over the last twenty-five years I have known many students who are similar to Tyrone. They want to make changes, they work hard to turn around their lives, and all the time they seem to be dealing with despair: a kind of despair that I believe some of the brightest, most articulate black men in my classroom fight each day. Tyrone's situation combines all the complexities of race, class, drugs, and a crumbling family structure that exist in our cities. In him, also, are hope, laughter, and the potential to be a great writer, college graduate, and Ph.D.

As I walk by him, huddled under his sweatshirt hood, I put my hand on his shoulder. He has the rental section of the *Star Tribune* open, looking at apartments. He glances up for a moment, meets my eye.

"Got to find a new crib." He turns back to the page where he has circled some of the ads. I stand with him for a moment longer, point to one or two he might be able to afford. He circles them, too.

The bell rings. Sheila continues to sleep. I go to her, whisper that it is time for first hour. She opens her eyes, shakes herself, stretches, gets ready to leave. Leah keeps writing at her computer. Tyrone starts out the door to go along to science.

I walk into the hall. I watch Ty head upstairs. So many students have given me such gifts over these years. Because these young people, black and white, Native and Asian, come back to my classroom again and again, after moving, after giving birth, after running away, they provide me with an unshakable faith. Because they keep trying to make it through the wall that Tyrone writes about, because they pull the hoods down from their faces, take off their sunglasses, begin to write, do math, study history, they continually reinforce my conviction that we cannot give up on *any* young people in this country.

HONESTY

Also, my students point out my mistakes and then forgive them, come back ready to write, to read with me.

One morning Leah was talking about her daughter, Jamika. She said that she needed to find some day care for her just for two days a week. I said something about welfare, asked if they gave her a voucher for day-care expenses.

"You think I take welfare, huh, Landsman? I don't take no welfare. My moms takes care of Jamika, 'cept now she got a job Mondays and Wednesdays. You think we all on welfare, huh, jus' cause we black and we got kids. You take welfare when you had your son?"

I told her, no, I didn't take welfare. And I was silent. She turned back to her computer that day, hurt. I apologized quietly and went back to my desk. I felt my face fall, my cheeks flush up. After all these years I still make classic mistakes in unsubtle ways, like the assumption of welfare, and in subtle ways, with a tone of voice, a gesture.

mistak happen

Leah came back the next day, full of stories, and showed me pictures of her child. She has always been good at starting over.

COMPLEXITY

Also, because students ask me to look at all sides of the prism, to see a picture, a person from all angles of light, they call up this story and thus give me a very personal gift:

In Dallas, Lillian, the woman who had talked to me about using the n-word in my rhyming, walked into the kitchen one morning, almost completely bald. Her husband had set fire to her hair. She had burnt, pink patches on her dark scalp. One shoulder was draped with a sling, her face was swollen, and she walked with a new limp. While my mother turned away, helpless, it was my father who took her to the hospital. When Lillian's husband called on our phone at midnight, at two in the morning looking for her, my father told this man that he would get a lawyer for her, that he would make sure she was safe, that he would pay the bills. And he did.

terribl

Many times I feel white liberals and even radicals, *talk* about what ought to change. Yet they rarely act. My father, for all his bigotry, did act. He followed through. And while these days his help might seem paternalistic, then it was what was needed and what Lillian asked for.

It has only been after working with the young men and women in my classroom, only after looking at them full and complex, in the sleepy mornings and hot afternoons of their lives, that I have been able to give the same full and fair scrutiny to my father. And I have seen some of the goodness that was there.

I believe he was often a bigot and a racist. I also believe that once in awhile he did what was right and that my inheritance from him may be a kind of activism that I never recognized before.

REFLECTION QUESTIONS

1. How much do you know about your students' lives? Their parents' struggles? Is it difficult for you to suspend judgment when working with students who do not speak or think as you do?
2. What is the difference for you between the act of *knowing* and *understanding*? What do you feel is necessary for us to begin to understand the lives of others who are not like us?
3. What are some mistakes you have made in relation to race or culture? What assumptions have you made and then been enlightened? What did you do? Give an example of a complex relationship with someone you know around the issue of race or class. Is there a way to handle this that lets you keep your friendship or connection and yet does not accede to racism or bigotry?

3

FIRST HOUR

Recognizing Oneself

Otto Spavek, you probably knew nothing about slavery, Jim Crow,
the W. E. B. and Booker T. Washington debate, Fred Douglass, Nat
Turner, jazz, blues or gospel, Civil Rights or Black Power. In turn, I
know nothing about howling blizzards and killer ice storms, diphthe-
ria, failed crops, farm foreclosure, loneliness and death on the prairie.
Otto Spavek, I'm thinking of you
exactly a hundred years after your birth.
I, a black man born in the City of Big Shoulders
a long way from here,
seven years before your death.
Standing here beside your grave,
in the grand scheme of the universe,
it's like we missed each other by just minutes
on the express train of American history.
The crows perched high atop the dead cottonwoods
unfurl their black wings like they have for a thousand years or so and
Seem to squawk at the thought of it.

—Philip Bryant, last two stanzas from poem
"Ottawa, MN, Cemetery—1992 In Memory of Otto Spavek"

Abell rings for the start of the hour. The halls are empty except for an occasional late student or a teacher hurrying to the office to get a phone call. Because I do not have an assigned class for this hour, I can leave and drive to a K–8 school nearby, where I have been a writer in residence for the last year. This is part of my dual job, as writer in the schools and teacher at ASP. Leah decides to stay and work in my room. She has no scheduled class this hour. I lock the door so that no one will bother her as she works. She can leave any time.

I walk into the parking lot and start toward Sheridan school. Today I will introduce David Haynes at an auditorium for seventh- and eighth-graders. They have read his novel *Right by My Side,* and he has agreed to talk about writing it and to have breakfast with some of them who have been selected for this honor because of their hard work on the novel and their written responses to it. I drive across the Mississippi River at Franklin Avenue. I keep going around the university and into Northeast Minneapolis, home to many Hmong, black, and Eastern European immigrants. This area of the city fought for years to keep its streets and its schools white. They used every trick in the book to maintain homogeneous schools. Finally, the demographics made such segregation impossible, and even the city councilmen and state representatives gave in to reality and stopped fighting the integration of the neighborhoods and schools in this section of Minneapolis.

As I park across from the school, three white men are drinking beer in their yard, working on their Harleys. Their arms are covered with tattoos and they smile as I get out of my Honda. This is my usual space, so we are all familiar to each other.

One of them shakes his head at my foreign car. "You gotta get a bigger car, you know."

"This is fine with me," I say as I lock the door.

"Ain't American, though," says another man who has stopped working on his bike for a moment.

"Aww man," the first man says. "Leave her alone. We'll watch this for ya so no one mess with it."

"Thanks," I say and head into Sheridan.

Because this neighborhood has only recently been integrated, I still feel much resentment and much tension in the air. These men are friendly to me. They assume we belong to the *same group,* the *white group.* But they are angry with the Hmong family newly arrived next door, and whose children run over their yard, and at times they have complained about them to me. Yet last week, I saw the same man who complained about the make of my car, holding a three-year-old Hmong boy in his arms, showing him the parts of his motorcycle, and then setting him gently on the seat. I sometimes feel that the simplest lesson in all this might be an acceptance of the intricacy and complexity of each one of us, that to generalize about anyone is unfair and destructive.

After signing in at the main office, I walk to the auditorium where David is talking to one of the teachers. He is a round man with glasses and coffee-colored skin. He has that nervous anticipation that most of us get before a reading. In this case, when the audience is composed of 160 seventh- and eighth-graders, there is much more nervousness than anticipation. David shifts from foot to foot as he talks to Jeff and Jehanne, the middle-school teachers. The kids file in, jostling, punching, and laughing.

About 40 percent of the students in the seventh and eighth grades are black, 30 percent Hmong, and 30 percent white. Ranging between the ages of eleven and fourteen, some kids are tall and gangly, over six feet, others short and compact. They are all hormones and questions, all distraction and bravado.

David, who was a middle-school teacher for years, watches as the kids take their seats and teachers move to sit strategically between the troublemakers.

As I introduce him to the audience, most of the kids settle down, become attentive. Some slump in the cushioned seats, others twirl their hair, a few whisper to friends until a hall aide leans across the row and asks them to be quiet. David smiles as he opens his book and begins to read aloud the first page of *Right by My Side*. The students laugh as he reads how Marshall, the protagonist, describes being the only black student in his social studies class:

> I walk into this class. World Literature for Sophomore Redneck Pinheads, I think they called it. Miss O' Hare is having Black Studies week in 1986 for the first time in her life, and if she flashed her nasty yellow teeth at me one more time, anyway, I'd have knocked them down her throat. We read—get this—excerpts from Tom Sawyer. Aunt Polly sends the nigra Jim to fetch Huck and Becky and Tom for victuals.
>
> Pinheads. Each and every one.

After only about fifteen minutes, David finishes reading the selection and asks for questions. Glancing at my watch, I am alarmed at his timing. How will he keep them from becoming restless and disruptive for forty-five more minutes?

"Why'd you use curse words in your book? My parents were upset I was reading a book with curse words." This comes from James, an African-American seventh-grader.

David walks toward James, holding onto the microphone. The room becomes very quiet.

"I wanted to make it real, the way Marshall would really talk. I know it might bother some people, but I want my books to seem like they really happen."

The students seem satisfied with his answer.

David goes further into the group, calling on kids, repeating their questions, answering them. He knows how to use his body, how to move, how to change his location among them to keep them interested.

"You always want to be a writer, from when you were little?" asks one young woman.

"I liked to read when I was little, but I never thought about being a writer until I was in college. Too much work." They laugh.

"You make a lot of money?" asks a boy who had been grabbing at his classmate's sweater while David was reading. David moves toward him.

"He asked if I made a lot of money being a writer," he says, looking around at his audience. "No. I worked at writing for ten years before I got anything published.

"Why you do it then?"

"Because I can't *not* do it." The kids look puzzled.

"Look," David says, standing back in front of them all, to take them in with his eyes, his arms, his whole body. "Aren't there some things you love to do, and you can't stand *not* to do them? Like eating candy if you see it, like playing soccer some nights after school? I just have to write. I am not happy unless I have some time to write."

The students are respectful, animated, focused. I have rarely seen them this attentive, not in all the times I have visited them as a writer myself.

I notice Travis, especially. He is a round young man, with skin identical to David's warm brown color, and he wears glasses. He has a look on his face that is different from any I have ever seen before. He seems satisfied, somehow, entirely content, yet vibrant. Some part of his body relaxes, settles in. He begins rattling off questions.

"What time do you get up? Do you think you had more problems because you're black? Did all these things in these books happen to you even though it is a novel and they don't have to have happened to you?"

"Wait a minute, man," says Travis's friend Nathan. "Let him answer one of them 'fore you go on askin' all them other questions!" The audience laughs. Travis looks nervous, waits.

David answers. "If it is not a day I have to be anywhere, like my job, or like at this school, I get up at noon. And I work until four in the morning on my best days. When I have to go to meetings or to my teaching, then I have to live like a normal person. Most of my life I have taken vacations to write. I am not sure if I have had a harder time because I am black, but it did take an awful long time for my books to be published. Now I have five published, though, so I am not sure about that. I think you always have to prove something more than white people have to prove if you are black. And no, not a lot of these things happened to me. I get ideas and characters and they just seem to take over and go where they want to go after awhile."

The students focus on David for the rest of the hour. He does a beautiful job, walking toward them, backing up, reading from his newest book: *Heathens*. When the assembly is over, the students give him a long round of applause.

Afterward, I take him upstairs to a classroom where he is to have breakfast with fifteen selected students. I stay to speak to them.

"You guys were great," I say. "Thanks for being such a fine audience. Good questions." They smile, duck their heads, or put their heads on the desks. Someone puts a CD in the disk player and turns the volume down. A regular rap beat becomes audible behind the bustle of the kids settling in, the sound of cars humming by on Broadway.

SEEING ONESELF

I turn to leave just as Travis opens the door to the room. He is carrying a pile of brown bag meals for this group.

"Hey, Travis. How you doing?" I ask.

He bursts out, "This is one of the happiest days of my life." I'm surprised. Often Travis is more withdrawn, somewhat whiny. But as I watch him settle into a seat across from David, suddenly I think I *see* why he feels the way he does.

Across from Travis sits himself. Across from Travis is a man who looks like him, who is an intellectual like him, and who is black like him. And I am sure David's blackness is crucial to the transfixed and joyous look on Travis's face.

[handwritten margin note: Happy the only]

Travis has often been teased by other students about being "too white," about being too smart, about not being hip enough or "black" enough. His teachers have told him that there are many black men who look like him, who are smart and studious and who do not lose their blackness. Now, I believe our words seem to make sense to him. He sees a black man who is smart and who studies and who is black, too, and something seems to have clicked for him, settled in in a pleasurable way. Watching him, his delight and joy, I find my throat closing, my eyes tearing. I am an old lady, I tell myself, and I get to be over-emotional. Travis's happiness is palpable, as it has never been before.

Perhaps his world has become resonant for just awhile here in this sun-filled classroom with the old wooden-framed windows, waxed floors, round tables, and the large poster of famous black abolitionists on the wall. Here he is, a round young black man with glasses, looking at a round middle-aged black man with glasses.

HEARING ONESELF

I head downstairs. I pass the auditorium again. Last week in this same auditorium I watched a Hmong theater performance with my ASP student Kai. She had asked me to bring her to see her brother perform.

I stop in and sit down for a moment in this huge room where David has just spoken. I am back at the play. Kai is beside me. A kindergarten class has filed in and a small Hmong boy sits on the other side of me. The room darkens. The kids are silent except for an underground hum of "shh's" and whispered "quiets!" Men and women come out on the stage dressed in bright costumes, some behind huge masks.

The opening five minutes of the play are in English. At first the child on my right is still. Then this boy, dressed in bright green and blue overalls and a yellow shirt, begins restlessly standing in his seat, turning to look behind him.

Suddenly, the characters begin speaking in Hmong, telling Hmong jokes. The boy freezes in his chair, turns around and becomes quiet, his eyes never leaving the stage. He remains transfixed, his hand reaching over to rest on my knee, his smile wide, and his eyes full of pure delight.

I suspect this is the first time he has heard his home language spoken on a stage before. And this language is part of an elaborate production, with costumes and moveable sets. Kai smiles at me, at him, laughing at the jokes, too.

Connecting

By the end of the performance the Hmong boy is sitting in my lap. Whenever the English is spoken, he becomes restless. Then, the Hmong, and he stops, his body resting against mine, his head thrown back against me in laughter when he hears the jokes.

As I look around, I notice that the white and black kids are a little uncomfortable. It is one of the first times they have been in a situation where they cannot understand what is being said and where the Hmong kids clearly understand and enjoy what they hear. It is interesting to watch the anger and annoyance build in whites and blacks who find themselves confused, even though the action on the stage tells almost all we need to know.

Note

Of course, the more we experience what others experience, including the feeling of exclusion and separation from the mainstream, the more we will understand others' feelings, the more we will empathize. Plays like this play are great for our students, not only for their artistic value, but for their emotional, experiential value. We learn what it is like to be "other" just for a short while.

Now, weeks later, as I get up out of my seat and head back to my car to drive to ASP for the day, I remember Kai's proud walk, the way she held herself so straight as we left the auditorium. She thanked me for taking her and asked how I liked it. I told her it was beautiful, with all that color and movement. I especially liked the paper dragon that was constantly on stage, and out of whose tail new characters emerged. She smiled and then became silent for the rest of the ride.

SENSING ONESELF

As I leave Sheridan to drive back across the river, I pass houses with elegant front porches next door to ones whose concrete foundations are crumbling. Dogs run free in this area of town. They appear in packs around the corners of apartment buildings.

I think about Travis, who lives on this block right near Sheridan. I remember again how he looked entranced as David talked about being a writer. We, as white people, tend to discount the power of the visual. Yet I know I remember things because I have *seen* them. Like many people I am a visual learner. We cannot, especially in this day and age, exaggerate the power of what we take in with our eyes. Our culture is based on this: television news, television shows, and films.

I have never forgotten the picture in *Life* magazine, 1960, of white women in hair curlers, crisscrossed bobby pins close to their scalps, shouting at the small black children trying to go to school in Little Rock, Arkansas. Their husbands stood next to them, shouting too. That was more than forty years ago and I can still see the way the mouths of these women seemed to stretch into snarls. They looked like cats, their backs arched, hissing. This picture is what I remember of those times, years before I marched into Montgomery, Alabama, to be with Martin Luther King. There is power in *seeing* that causes us to understand evil and sorrow, causes us to know with our bodies what we might not know yet with our minds. I felt when I looked at those angry men and women and the children who were trying to walk by them to get to school, their eyes staring straight ahead, the absolute rightness of these students' cause. I do not believe this event in history would have had the impact on me that it had if I had just read about it. Now, being older, I have also tried to understand the complexity of the lives of those men and women doing the shouting.

The power of the visual can transport students into the realm of possibilities for themselves. If previously students never saw their own future *embodied* in a writer, an engineer, a pilot, or a doctor of their own race, once they have talked with and *seen* such people in the classroom, they can conceive of such a future for themselves. They must experience visual and visceral connections to believe in them.

And this is cumulative. That Travis or Kai had this one experience, or maybe three or four just like it, bears its weight lightly compared to the thousands of times there were no black or Hmong faces in sight. During David's talk, the fact that the black kids in that auditorium felt connected in a visceral way to someone standing at the podium should not minimize the endless mornings and afternoons in classrooms where white teachers talk about white people, white writers, white scientists, and white heroes.

EVERY DAY

From the time they were babies, I wish our students saw the faces of people with their skin color and of their ethnicity in movies and on calendars, on postcards and in film. What a difference it would make if voices with a dialect, accent, and language like their own were part of their school lives from kindergarten on. And such pictures, such voices, would not be segregated to one part of the school, the month, or the year. They would be there all year round, woven into the everyday: of doors-opening-bells-ringing-large-orange-buses-pulling-up-to-the-brick-building-in-the-dead-of-a-winter-night-morning.

James Banks breaks down the ways schools try to involve the perspectives of people who are not European American into the classroom in his articles and books on schools. This quote from an article in the *Multicultural Leader* defines the Transformative Approach, as differentiated from the Contributions and Additive Approaches. It is important for us to be aware of the differences and to work toward a more integrated and complex approach to educating all students in our classrooms. *yes*

> This [Transformative] approach changes the basic assumptions of the curriculum and enables students to view concepts, issues, themes and problems from several ethnic perspectives and points of view. The key curriculum issue involved in the Transformative Approach is not the addition of a long list of ethnic groups, heroes, and contributions, but the infusion of various perspectives, frames of reference, and content from various groups that will extend students' understandings of the nature, development, and complexity of U.S. society. . . .
>
> When studying U.S. history, language, music, arts, science, and mathematics, the emphasis should not be on the ways in which various ethnic and cultural groups have "contributed" to mainstream U.S. society and culture. The emphasis, rather, should be on how the common U.S. culture and society emerged from a complex synthesis and interaction of the diverse cultural elements that originated within the various cultural, racial, ethnic, and religious groups that make up American society.

I would add to this definition of transformative and include the importance of advocating for the hiring of teachers, administrators, and counselors of color so that our students see a variety of adults *teaching* such a complex and diverse curriculum. In addition to transforming our curriculum to include many perspectives not represented in our traditional texts, our schools and classrooms might become places where such perspectives are *embodied* by actual people standing in front of the class or, even better, sitting in small groups with our students, telling their stories.

It also seems just as important for young people in suburban schools to see before them people of color in all aspects of their day. For all of us, it means making space and time for people who are black, Asian, Latino/a, and Native to become part of our rooms. There is something artificial about having a once-a-year visit by a black doctor. It is better than nothing, yet I think we need to go further: call up friends, contact universities, create whole programs for *integrating* people of color, as well as differing perspectives, into our educational institutions.

Young people see through anything that is false or halfway there. They will catch us being dismissive, will know if we are cursory or insincere. And so the presence of people of color in classrooms and in buildings, on school boards and in administration, must be encouraged with all the joy and welcome such an initiative requires.

The result can be a change in the way our students, and we ourselves, look at the world. The result can prepare us whites, and our white children especially, for the years ahead when we will be working more and more with those whose skins are not like our own.

I pull up to the parking lot behind ASP. As I walk around to the front of the building, I see Sarah, a white student from my fifth hour, standing across the street, waiting for a bus.

"Where are you going?" I shout. "Aren't you going to be in my class today?"

She runs across the street and wraps her arms around my waist, puts her head on my shoulder. I can smell her sweet marijuana smell, her little girl sweat smell, her grown-up perfume smell all at once.

"I can't handle it today, Landsman. I need to get me some more money. Okay?"

She smiles and looks in my eyes, turns my face to hold it in her hands.

"Don't take it personal now, Landsman. I may be back fifth hour; then I'll come in and read my book."

I take her hands from my face and hang on to them. I hate to let her go.

"You come back."

She drops my hands and turns to go across to the other side of the street again. A clean, tight sweater covers her thin shoulders, and her high-top shoes are scuffed white. Her jeans are also clean and snug around her body. She has actually done some modeling, never telling her employer that she lives on the street. Sarah made me a map of Minneapolis in class one day. She drew in symbols for all the safe places for getting food, for sleeping, for using the bathrooms, if you were homeless. She is one of those students who keeps me up at night, her image before me at 2 A.M. when I wake up suddenly, anxious.

She waves from the window of the bus as I start up the steps to school.

INCLUDING THE WOMEN

I think of Sarah when I think of the *invisibility* of women in the curriculum, in the literature of our schools. Even women with my white skin are rarely present in history texts. We are not often seen as people who "made" history. We sat by the sides of the men who drove the wagon trains. We lifted great iron pots off stoves in those always cozy-looking homes on the prairie; and we sewed buckskin "breeches" (whatever they were) for our men who went out on horseback with lariats and roped cattle for our living.

Our students might learn of *unusual* women, like Abigail Adams, who challenged the sexism of the new Constitution, or Marie Curie, who was a physicist and helped discover radium. However, these are still often seen as exceptions to the *usual* women, the ones in the background. White men are still portrayed as the main movers of history because history is often defined in masculine terms: battles, surrenders, treaties, conquests. Men's work is seen as work, women's work is seen as women's work.

In advanced-placement English classes—classes Sarah could easily pass if she was a traditional student—she would still read 90 percent of books written by white British men, all of whom have passed away. Right now, Sarah is reading books by Ursula Leguin, a science fiction writer who is not an "easy read" but rather someone who writes in complex sentences, complicated plots, and with lots of detail. For awhile, Sarah could not get enough of Zora Neale Hurston, an African-American author who wrote during the Harlem Renaissance. Sarah read all Hurston's novels and her autobiography. Yet I never sense that for her this reading connects, or has ever connected, with what she does in school. She just tells me she is grateful for public libraries, where you can get books anywhere in the city and leave them off anywhere you happen to be living.

Right now, Sarah has too much to do to make school her priority. It has never made her a priority in its panoply of photographs, in its collections of literature. I know we have come a ways, yet I feel such sorrow when I watch the Sarahs of our classes. She brings back to me my own fear of sports. Even though I loved running, I was afraid that participating in athletics would make me too masculine. I never pictured myself as a doctor. Rather, I toyed with the idea of being a nurse until I fainted in the sixth grade when giving a report on the Red Cross. While for some women choosing an unusual career has become easier, for others, who get their information from television and the movies, powerful stereotypes still limit them.

change

Yet despite the limited role of white women in literature and history texts, at least white students see men with their same skin color as the makers of history. They *see* men who look like their fathers or brothers as part of the forces that created this country. Black women are twice invisible in this scenario, by their skin and by their gender. A young black woman can graduate from many of our schools without having the slightest hint that she was shaping the world. She hears nothing about her writing *Beloved,* nothing about her civil rights work, and nothing about her way with small children as a pediatrician, or the fact that she saved lives on battlefields. How twice missed she is . . . a black woman who cannot see her men and cannot see herself or even her white sisters in the world.

I want to change this soon. I want to wave a wand and make deep curriculum and pedagogic changes that will bring about a true inclusion of women into our schools. I feel an urgency about all this as I see Sarah trying to get modeling jobs in dangerous places, or Sheila taking on all the responsibility for a child, almost giving up on college.

In person and in our texts, I want to present the people who created this country, so that Sarah, Leah, Tyrone, Travis, and all students can feel a connection to the education we offer them. And so that they can feel hope, something they lack altogether on their worst days.

REFLECTION QUESTIONS

1. In your school where you grew up, or in the school where you teach, do or did students "see themselves" in the teachers, staff, and administration around them? What might be done to connect students to those who look like them?

2. Why do you think it is essential for students to see or hear themselves in the schools in which they attend? Have you ever been in a situation where you are surrounded by a group of people who do not look or sound or act like you?

3. Put into your own words what Transformative Curriculum and Teaching might be? Give examples.

4. Without discounting the power of race, what do you notice about the role of women in the curriculums and content of instruction in our schools? Is understanding this a *way in* to understanding the absence of people of color and their perspectives in our schools?

4

SECOND HOUR
History and Literature

This fact faced, with all its implications, it can be seen that the history of the American Negro problem is not merely shameful, it is also something of an achievement. For even when the worst has been said, it must also be added that the perpetual challenge posed by this problem was always, somehow, perpetually met. It is precisely this black–white experience which may prove of indispensable value to us in the world we face today. This world is white no longer, and it will never be white again.

—James Baldwin

WORKING-CLASS INVISIBILITY

I walk toward my classroom. Josh, another white student, is waiting for me at the door. He had attended school sporadically before he started with us, often preferring to smoke dope, burglarize homes, or work at his job in the Mega Mall instead of coming to class. In the six months he has been at ASP, he has missed only one week. He waves as I head toward him.

Josh also is not talked about in the books he reads: not men like his father, who worked in the kitchens or on the loading dock, or his mother, standing beside some customer in a restaurant, taking down his order for chef's salad and iced tea. So many of the parents of the students I teach are absent from our texts.

The working white and black men on their hands and knees laying wire for the new concert hall are not shown in our history books. The Native-American men who hang up above the others in the balcony, adjusting the velvet on the box seats, and the white women who climb to install the chandeliers: they are nowhere to be seen when we look at pictures of the elegant hall.

Working people are rarely seen except during pictures of the Depression, in bread lines. Until recently, these men and women have been absent from our understanding of the forces of history. Only in publications like *Rethinking Schools,* an educators' forum for changing the way schools work, and in some new, daring textbooks, do we see any attempt to give voice to the silence, presence to the absence, of so many.

HISTORY AS A COMPLEXITY OF TRUTHS

As I open the door to my room, Josh follows me in.

"People are going to be comin' in here all pissed off."

"Why?" I ask. Then I remember that a speaker has been here this morning. It was one of the reasons I could actually leave the building to be at Sheridan without having to worry about getting back exactly on time.

Just then Demetrius, a new student this hour, comes into my room, sits down, and stares sullenly at the wall.

"What did the speaker talk about?" I ask.

"Slaves and shit like that," says Demetrius. He puts his head on his hands. He is a light-skinned young black man with blue eyes and a large Afro haircut.

"He talked about baggy pants and stuff. Like where they came from in slavery times," says Josh, who heads over to get his disk out of the holder at the front of the room.

"He don't know shit!" Demetrius leans back now and folds his arms across his chest.

"He told how blacks were forced to shuffle into church with no belts on, so their pants rode low. You know, to humiliate them." Josh says this as he goes over to the couch and sits down.

I take off my purse and put it in my desk drawer. Tyrone comes in. He gets out his disk and walks over to his usual place at a computer. He is working on his autobiography and seems intent on getting to it now. He looks at Demetrius.

"Why you so pissed, man? He jus' telling you stuff that's true."

"He don't know shit. Sayin' we look like some ol' slaves."

Tyrone shakes his head. He looks intently at his screen, scrolls it through, and reads what is there.

I do not approach Demetrius right now. I have seen this many times: the anger and volatility of discussions about slavery. Often, speakers come in for an hour, drop some interesting bit of history, filled with graphic detail and important facts, on the students, and then leave. And what they say is true, yet there is no context, nothing leading up to these quick lessons, these fill-in forty-five-minute sessions that are supposed to count as African-American history lessons. And we teachers, most of us white, are left with the discomfort, the hostility that comes after such talks. I am tired of these quick fixes, a superficial attempt to right a more complex wrong in our education system. Also, I do not feel on firm ground here, afraid I will say the "wrong thing."

I find that black students often do not want to be reminded of their ancestors' arrival here. Without a context, without time to understand, read, and write, it seems too big, too powerfully melancholy for many students to understand. Rather than being presented with a cursory description of slavery, they seem to want to avoid any discussion of it altogether.

Also, there are aspects of slavery and of those times that are entirely left out of these presentations: slave insurrections, successful lives of runaway slaves, whole countries run by Africans. Because the study of slavery is often simplistic, the little bits of truth thrown out to our students by the most well-meaning visitors often provoke intense anger. Coupled with our own hesitancy as white teachers to talk about such issues, these auditoriums or assemblies can create more problems than they help to remedy.

In many American History textbooks, even today, when I come across a picture of slaves on the auction block, of lynchings in Mississippi, the text makes me think all *that*—the ugliness of auctions of human beings, the hanging of men and women, the runaways—*all that* has ended. Rarely is there time given in the lesson plans, or in the text itself, for a discussion of the lasting effects of this history, effects that influence the way people think, act, and perceive themselves and others today.

When we read these texts, we simply turn the page, go on to World War I, maybe, or Thomas Edison and his fine inventions.

Civilization has almost always been defined in such textbooks as something built, written, composed, *completed* by white men. It is always a finished product. While symphonies were *art*, jazz, with its improvisation, scat singing, and unexpected long solos when the mood came on, was *entertainment*. Rarely do our students see improvisation as part of culture. And along with this, history is rarely seen as a constantly changing field, with new discoveries being made all the time, discoveries that can change the way events and phenomena from years ago are perceived today.

It is only at this point in my life, when I am in my fifties, that I have learned of black cowboys and cowgirls settling the West, Jewish farmers, or the spread of gospel music. I have read new approaches to history, attended plays at the black repertory theater nearby, and watched documentaries about the Tuskegee airmen. Yet such presentations of facts are not in many of the books in our public schools—not in the ones Demetrius has read or in the schools where Josh has studied. What of the railroad men, the porters and the waiters, and the careful way someone holds a door?

In order to hold our students' attention, I believe that the continuum of history—its influence on present-day economics, politics, neighborhoods, and the law—must be presented in all its multifaceted complexity. I believe I speak here about nothing less than presenting the truth, *in its difficult and troublesome entirety.*

As white teachers, then, we must be ready to advocate for a change in the way history is taught. Important questions must be asked that have to do with morality, with compassion, with how decisions have been made and by whom. The important question "In whose interest?" was a thing done, a book published, a law passed must be a part of our students' and our own contemplation of what has formed our past. Once I have begun to ask this single question, I have thought differently about so much: history, politics, and power.

I have often wondered what would happen if for one year, we tried having a White Studies Month. And except for that month, white people, their contributions to the world, their exploits, and their discoveries would rarely be mentioned, would not be part of the curriculum.

Leah comes in now, strangely calm. She is usually one of those students who reacts the most negatively to these quickie history lectures.

"Hey, Landsman!" She smiles. I smile back at her, and she heads for her computer. I hand her her disk and she inserts it. Up comes her autobiography. She must have added three or four sentences to it after I left her alone first hour. She leans down and pulls a sandwich out of her bag. I smell the sweet smell of marijuana on her.

"Did you go to the assembly?" I ask her.

"Nah, Landsman. I don't need to hear any of that slavery shit." She smiles again.

Demetrius looks up, "You got that right, girl."

Tyrone is concentrating on his work, ignoring the conversation.

"It's just him tellin' you about your people," says Josh, still sitting on the couch, not interested in getting to work.

"They ain't my people," says Demetrius. "My homies my people. That's it."

"I hear that," says Leah, still squinting at her story.

Tyrone looks up from his computer screen. "They *was* your people, though."

"Don't care about nothin' that *was*. I got nothin' 'cept my life today, that white people have messed up. No offense, Landsman." Leah says this, not fully involved in the conversation. It has always been interesting to me that their referring to white people is seen as a possible insult to me, as though I might be offended at something negative said about my "race."

"Yeah. But it's good to know how all this happened. They just tryin' to tell our story in this school. Not jus' the white story." Tyrone speaks and then immediately turns back to the computer.

"Not *all* white people did all that shit," Josh says.

The statement goes out into the room, up for grabs. I watch him closely. He shrugs his shoulders. He looks unusually thin in his plaid shirt, baggy pants, and Timberland boots. His clothes hang on him.

"Okay, man, now don't get your white ass upset. We know that, man." Tyrone says this, smiling at Josh. Josh smiles back.

Josh is usually smiling. He is also unafraid of conversations like this one. I find a lot of young white men like this, ready to ask questions, listen, tease, and back off whenever necessary. Along with the Tyrones and the Sheilas, it is these young white men and women, the ordinary, middle- and working-class white students at regular schools, who give me hope, too.

I do not want to seem like a Pollyanna here, however. At ASP there is also a group of white students who want to have nothing to do with the black students in the building, who make racist statements, and who wear clothes that indicate their attachment to the White Power movement. We have a lot to do to reach these young men and women. In our more affluent suburbs there are similar young men, who at times become dangerous, as Littleton, Colorado, shows. I do find it interesting that with all the fear of "inner city schools" or "inner city neighborhoods," it is not here that the most violent incidents involving young people have happened. It is in our primarily white outer ring suburbs, or small towns, where mass shootings occur.

SEARCHING FOR
WHITE ANTIRACIST HEROES

As I watch Josh, reading over his paper one more time, I wonder if, even though he is a young white man, he feels connected to the history we have presented to him over the years. I wonder if he feels a great identity with the literature he has been asked to read. I don't think so.

For Josh, for all our students, we need a new panoply of fine men and women. We need to present white heroes whom our students have never envisioned as heroes before: labor union leaders, civil rights workers, courageous judges. It seems to me it is vital to add to our definition of history the history of antiracism. In addition to stories of black, brown, Native, and Asian heroes, we need to include stories of white people who stood next to their brothers and sisters of color to create a more just society. We do not need to romanticize them, but we can present them in all their complexity, all their imperfections.

We teach much *in isolation.* For high school students this does not work. Whether we like it or not, whether our education was a classical one or not, it is time to recognize that we need to hook our students, gather them in. What can be powerful, then, is to use stories of community organizers today and compare them to the stories of those who worked in the Warsaw ghetto. This can provide a way into the history of that time. Connecting the life of John Lewis, the civil rights leader and present-day congressman from Georgia, and the life of Pastor Trocme, the man who organized his town in the French Alps to save thousands of Jewish children, makes both of these men real to students in my classes.

This history of resistance to oppression is an exciting way to reach students. By including such heroes, black and white, we can certainly engage more of our students in the curriculum, as part of a meaningful education.

"Why you mad at all white people?" Josh asks quietly from his position on the couch.

Leah responds to Josh's question. "'Cause I see white people faces and I just get mad." She leans back in her chair, taking a bite out of her sandwich and drinking a long drink of Dr. Pepper.

"It ain't jus' white people mess you up, man. It's your own people. You know what I'm talkin' about." This from Tyrone.

"What you sayin', man?"

Tyrone shakes his head. "Who you think sold them slaves to them white people, man?"

"More white people, *that* who." Demetrius has an edge to his voice now. He looks at me nervously, looks back at Tyrone. "You shouldn't be talkin' 'bout this, man."

"You the one started talking about it, man." Tyrone stands up.

Demetrius stands up. I step between them. Tyrone sits down, shakes his head, and picks up the newspaper. Demetrius stays standing behind me, muttering. I don't know him well enough to know what to say. Leah watches.

"Oooooh, Landsman. They gonna get into it." She smiles.

"No, they're not." I motion for Demetrius to sit down and he does. I walk over to him, ask him to get started on his writing. He crosses his arms over his chest, stares at the screen. I do not try to force him, even now. He is probably taking the most sensible way out: sitting in silence until he cools down.

I leave him and go over to Leah. She turns back to her story.

"See what happens when they bring those people in talkin' slave shit." She looks up at me.

"They just tellin' stuff that's true." This comes from Josh, who has finally settled down at a computer in the corner of the room, his favorite, private spot.

"Please, Josh, just go on and get to work." He clicks on the screen and begins rereading his assignment. I could have responded sooner: to what Tyrone said, to how Demetrius responded. I am still unsure of myself when it comes to these discussions some days. I am not sure, either, who Demetrius is, what he wants from this class or from me, his white teacher. What always bothers me, though, is the fact that these students have not always had discussions about slavery in their history classes, in their social studies courses, before they arrived here at ASP.

There *is* a history of African complicity in the slave trade. And this aspect of the situation is very tricky. Because textbooks and curriculum planners do not go into this part of history with any detail, because they do not discuss the differences between slave systems in Africa and the United States, teachers are unaware of how to talk to students about such complicity without creating a firestorm. After all, they have received the same simplistic instruction on the history of slavery as that of their students. An insightful paragraph from James W. Loewen's book

Lies My Teacher Told Me demonstrates the complexity of this issue and the importance for teachers and students to understand the history of slavery in the world and the different form of slavery in the United States.

> Slavery existed in many societies and periods before and after the African slave trade. Made possible by Europe's advantages in military and social technology, the slavery started by Europeans in the fifteenth century was different, because it became the enslavement of one *race* by another. Increasingly, whites viewed the enslavement of whites as illegitimate, while the enslavement of Africans became acceptable. Unlike earlier slaveries, children of African American slaves would be slaves forever and could never achieve freedom through intermarriage [with] the owning class. The rationale for the differential treatment was racism.

This might have been a good time for me to talk about this. I do not do it. At another time, without the volatility of a new student in the class, I might have stopped what we were doing and discussed this topic of complicity. Instead I move on, separate my students, and miss a chance to hold a good discussion.

I ask Leah if I can read what she has written. She puts her hand over the screen. "Not yet, Landsman, I got to finish it before I let you see it."

Finally, they are all working except Demetrius. The sun is pouring through the windows. A siren wails outside, coming closer. Then it becomes faint as the squad car moves past our building and on up River Street. Not one of the students moves at the sound. No one goes to look out, to see what is happening. I am always slightly surprised by their lack of reaction. I cannot resist walking over to that side of the room myself, looking down, watching the squad car move in and out of the cars that have pulled over, then drive through the red light and disappear. I turn back to my desk as Tyrone holds up his hand. I walk over to where he is sitting.

After he finished reading *Makes Me Wanna Holler*, Tyrone asked me for *Native Son* by Richard Wright, because that was the book that McCall said turned him around in prison. He has just finished this.

"I gotta be done now, right, Landsman? You gotta give me my credit now, right?"

"No way," I tell him. "You haven't read any women yet. Time for the women writers." I am not sure if I am imagining it, but he looks somewhat relieved.

"Oh man, you doggin' me." He shakes his head.

"What you wanna do, be called a sexist?" I ask.

He laughs. "Wouldn't tell you if I did."

I hand him Gloria Naylor's *Women of Brewster Street*. He shakes his head.

"Okay now, man. This is May. You know this is the last one."

I smile. "We'll see. You still need this credit to graduate now, don't you?"

"Don't dog me, Landsman."

"Now would I do that?"

"Yep." He opens the book and starts to read.

Tyrone's essay on Nathan McCall's book included something like this:

> He [Nathan McCall] came to the conclusion that all whites weren't as racist as he had once thought, and that many were insecure about racism. . . . Many whites don't know how to interact with blacks because they were never taught. Whites run the country but know almost nothing directly about other cultures except what other whites teach them. The school system has failed them as much as it has failed us. Racism is a problem in this country but it will not be dealt with until we confide in each other to fix this ancient problem.

I think of this passage each day I work with Tyrone. His words belie the media image of a young black man, ex-gangster, former burglar. His words challenge the stereotype of the angry black man who cannot see anything from anyone else's point of view. This passage is simply Tyrone, thinking on the page, *after reading a book where he saw himself.* This passage reveals a generous heart, which is as much part of the picture of Ty as his hooded sweatshirt, his hip hop CDs, and his sullen mornings.

His experience with *Makes Me Wanna Holler* recalls the words Sekou Sundiata, a poet, spoke in an interview with Bill Moyers. Sundiata says to Moyers, his smile and eyes lighting up the camera and his red shirt warm in the sun that streams in the window:

> My experience of my humanity first came through black culture—through the language, through the church, through the neighborhood, through all of that— and when I started hearing those poets, they spoke to that. Amiri Baraka had a poem called "With Your Badd Self." I didn't know you could say that in a poem. I mean, we said that all the time in the neighborhood, but he was saying it in a poem.
>
> There was a hit song by James Brown which had that line, so it was a slang term but this man made literature out of it and that really enabled me. *It opened up a door and said, "Wait a minute! There's poetry in the language I speak. There's poetry, therefore, in my culture, and in this place."* [italics mine]

I grew up in the projects and we never reflected on the projects, we just lived in them, but Victor Hernandez Cruz and other poets started writing about the projects and people in the neighborhood. So here was some reflection, some introspection. Their poems named the world in particular ways and *foregrounded things that in school were in the background or in the margins or even outside.* [italics mine] That's how I discovered that there's poetry in the language I know and the culture I know.

I want, more than anything as a teacher, to bring to the foreground the poetry in the language of my students. I believe that doing this is absolutely essential for building a complete picture for all students of the way men and women of color have written about, built, talked about, and made this country, through literature, labor, art, and daily struggle.

RIGHTING THE WRONG OF SILENCE

Before he came upon McCall's book, Tyrone had read very few black authors: not in the years of his growing up, his years in middle school, or regular high school. And before our talks about language, I never truly understood the power of the *silences:* the *lack* of black literature, the *absence* of runaway slaves in our curriculums. This omission is not just an omission of Tyrone's past, of his culture; it is silence surrounding all of our history.

Even now, we often do not notice absences. We do not think to look for those who do not look like us. This seems to be an unconscious arrogance that accompanies the power of skin color: the assumption of our place at the center of the world. On those mornings when I see a young black girl surreptitiously rub her hand along the pictures of black women in the book *To Dream a World,* I wonder: Is it asking too much to include them all? Is it too much to ask our schools to encompass the mixture of all these kids' lives, in what they read, in whom they see? And my frustration, even my anger, is to realize, every day, in different contexts, that we are not even close to including them.

If we changed our curriculum to welcome all students, to include the history of all of us, women, people of color, working-class men and women, antiracists, would this give Demetrius hope? It might. Would Tyrone's life be easier? I am not naive enough to think that it would be. What I believe our schools can do, however, is simply to right *part,* the part we have control over, of a complex wrong: the complex wrong of the racism that still pervades the policies, the economics, the legal system, and personal interactions in this country.

Ty is reading Naylor now, already lost in the book. Leah is restless, reaching in her purse for her wallet, playing with her lipstick. Demetrius is staring at his computer, not moving. His jaw is working, I can see the muscle bulge against his gold skin. I walk over to him.

"Need help getting started?" I ask. He shrugs his shoulders. I find a different short story than the one he is reading, one that might appeal more to him. It is actually an excerpt from the McCall book. He begins reading it and focuses on the page. I leave him.

LITERATURE: INTERWEAVING

We can find books and music, find pictures and poems, colors and figures in history. This, in itself, is not complicated: to make their own history and literature visible and audible to America's children.

Doing this is not about playing rap music in the classroom. We can bring in the sound and poetry of that music, certainly. But even better, we can tie the imagery and the rhythm in rap to the imagery in a sonnet, the rhythm in a poem by Keats. We might want to connect the themes in the Fugees' latest CD to the intricate plays of Shakespeare. Then we can talk about the way artists hide their meanings, how we can find them. As I watch the best teachers do this, I am dazzled by the possibilities.

The hour will be over in ten minutes. Leah gets up and walks to the door. She yells down the hall to someone. I step beside her.

"Go on back and sit down, now. You have ten minutes left."

"Aww, Landsman I can't do no more work right now." She waves at two young men who are coming up the hallway.

"Hey, man, what you doin' here?" she asks.

A tall boy with a gold tooth and dark skin smiles.

"I goin' here now. You know that."

"You ain't goin' to no ASP."

"Yeah I am, baby. You know that."

I realize that these two young men may not go to our school. Just as I am about to ask them who their teacher is, a hall guard comes down the hall walking fast.

"You two gotta leave *now!*" He fingers the beeper on his waist. "I ain't messin' with you, now, you gotta get out this school."

I gently put my hand on Leah's shoulder, turn her, and pull my door closed as we both go into the room. This does not always work, but Leah seems to want to stay out of anything that might happen with these two. I sit beside her as she slumps on the couch in the back of the room.

Josh comes back there with us. He hands me a new part of his autobiography. He stands waiting for me to read it.

I think that there are two reasons why I am alive. One of them is that I haven't done everything that I wanted to do in my life yet. Some of those things are moving out on my own, finishing high school, getting my license, having my own car, and getting a full-time job. The other reason has to do with my real father. It took him fourteen years and it took me to get shot before he would come and visit me.

I tell Josh it is good, that he has captured the way some events have a strange way of bringing us gifts when we least expect them. He asks me if he is done with it.

"Just one more round. Look for punctuation. And create a scene between your father and you, in the hospital."

He takes it back and stands, musing over it for a moment. A few months ago he would have been angry at the work I am asking him to do on this one piece of writing. Today, he is mellow. He is also thinking of using this piece of writing in an application for a community college.

Leah shakes her head. "Why you wanna dog us, Landsman? Makin' us do it over all the time?"

"I want it perfect."

"No way. Nothin' perfect."

She picks up a copy of *Essence* and begins to look through it. I leave her, go to my desk, take attendance for this past hour. I am missing five students. This is not unusual in this school. I don't like it, though. I don't even know some of the kids whose names are on my list. They have come one time and have not returned. Some may have gone back to the school that kicked them out. Some may not go to school at all. They might show up in my classroom one day, ready to work, stay a few weeks, and drift off. I don't know how to hold them.

I feel my heart drop for an instant. My breath catches. I can see these young people, alone on the street perhaps, or working at the car wash on University

Avenue. There are poets in those places, scientists at McDonald's. Many of them are not white but Latino/a, Indian. I miss them with a strange longing. It is a longing to know them. I want to get my hands on them, to give them words or music, something that will bring that sudden glint of delight into their eyes, the way it might have been when they started with us, in first grade, arriving in the classroom, eager and hungry.

LITERATURE:
COUNTERING PEER PRESSURE TO FAIL

Next period starts in a minute. I tell Tyrone, Josh, and Demetrius to put away their disks in the holder, to get ready to leave. Leah has not come to the front of the room. She will be in my next hour today, Mom's Writing Class day, and so she stays back. The rest get up slowly, move toward the door, and open it. They stand there until I will let them go.

"Where you workin', man?" Demetrius asks Tyrone.

"Over northeast. Post office."

"You been there long?"

"A year."

"Man. You makin' money?"

"Enough."

"Yeah. What's enough, man?"

"Enough." Tyrone does not meet Demetrius's eye. He leans against the doorsill looking out into the hall.

"Chicken shit job. Probably don't make no money."

"He makes money, man." This comes from Josh. "Post office jobs pay decent."

"Yeah." Demetrius does not look at Josh. They all become silent. I tell them they can go. As I stand in the hall, I see Ty walk toward the stairway to his science class. He will be challenged at least five or six times before he leaves school. Someone will mock his regular job, his attendance in class, his desire to graduate. It is one of the toughest challenges he has to meet, other black students who want him to skip, smoke dope, or fight.

There are a lot of Tyrones I see walking these halls, a lot of Demetriuses. And I want the Tyrones to win, the Demetriuses to change. For us, as teachers, this is our toughest challenge, too. We are constantly in the position of trying to counter the influence of our students' own peer group. I believe one way to do this is to provide strength, hope, and support enough so that students find the power to resist the pull to quit, drop out, hang out, make a quick buck somewhere else. In addition to keeping these students in class, we find ourselves in meetings with their parents, their pastors, their advocates—important elders who are trying to keep them there, too.

This is at the heart of what we are doing and at the heart of what will turn around the failure rates of students of color, and an increasing number of white students, in this country and in our cities. Because I am seeing an increasing temptation to skip, quit, drop out in white schools, too. I am seeing the pressure on white students to do poorly on tests. They, too, do not want to be heckled by their peers for being too smart.

I have often wondered where this negative peer pressure comes from. I know that "nerds" have been harassed in schools for centuries. Yet I also know that twenty years ago more parents and more students of all cultures believed that getting a good education was the key to making it in this country. I do not find this to be the case today. Many of my students cannot see themselves in college or even vocational school after graduating from high school. The numbers of African-American students who do not pass basic skills tests in my own school system is too high to ignore. Yet the whole time I am writing this, I am aware that even to state the problem calls up stereotypes.

Beverly Tatum, in her book *Why Are All the Black Kids Sitting Together in the Cafeteria,* speaks about this phenomenon:

> Unfortunately for Black teenagers, [those] cultural stereotypes do not usually include academic achievement. Academic success is more often associated with being White. During the encounter phase of racial identity development, when the search for identity leads toward cultural stereotypes and away from anything that might be associated with Whiteness, academic performance often declines. Doing well in school becomes identified as trying to be White. Being smart becomes the opposite of being cool.

How do we address an identifiable problem, one that in some instances is more prevalent in one or two cultures, without insinuating that it is racially or culturally determined? I believe we have to look at what the systems in this country have done to contribute to the situation. How have we inadvertently reinforced the negative self-images of those students who are black or Latino/a?

Why is academic success seen as a "white thing"? Have we, as white educators, assumed certain things about the futures of students of color, and have we unconsciously communicated lower expectations to them? How have the neighborhood, the community, and the church responded to a student's behavior?

I believe we have to talk openly with those who are part of the students' environment, part of all that surrounds them, to find some answers to what is happening in our schools. We are responsible for our place, our curriculum, our teaching styles, and the experiences we can provide in our rooms. We are responsible for the way we treat students, for how much we expect from them. The communities in which these students live are responsible also, for reaching out to them, for reading to them when books are available, for encouraging them to do homework.

I always come back to the necessity for white men and women who are the leaders in this country to recognize the deep-seated inequality in our school systems and in our economic structure. It is our job to encourage such recognition by our actions, by our instruction, and by our commitment to change it. Part of this commitment can manifest itself in providing support for students who are trying to avoid the pressure to fail, and in pushing those students who are caught up in such failure, to conceive of their lives differently.

REFLECTION QUESTIONS

1. At the end of the Baldwin quote in the epigraph to this chapter, he states, "This world is white no longer and will never be white again." How relevant is this to our world today? How will it, or does it, affect your classroom, your neighborhood, your daily life at work or in your community?
2. Describe some ways you could counter many textbooks, which are often written from a white male perspective. Because we are trying to describe what is *not there*, this can be tricky. Where could you find other points of view?
3. When you learned about history, did you learn about contemporary white antiracist heroes or heroines? What do you think would happen if we had a designated "White History Month"? What would the reaction be?
4. Instead of marginalizing people of color into Black History Month, or Black Poets unit, how can we interweave all people into the curriculum?

CHAPTER 4

What themes might we use? How can we take advantage of music, art, or other disciplines?

5. Can you think of ways that connecting to student lives could disrupt the idea that education is a "white thing"? How could this disrupt peer pressure among students of color not to buy into education? How does this kind of anti-school pressure play out in primarily white schools?

5

THIRD HOUR

Student Voices as the Center of the Class

All we own, at least for the short time we have it, is our life.
With it we write what we come to know of the world.

—Alice Walker, *Anything We Love Can Be Saved*

I like

Leah calls from the back of the room, "What we doin' in here this time? Writin'?"

"'Course we writin'," says Sheila, who has come in now. "That's why it's called Mom's Writin' Class!"

Leah smiles then. More of them file in, young women, all parents of babies or toddlers. This is my favorite hour of the week.

We gather around the table in the center of the room. The sun comes in on them all, and on the notebooks with their purple, green, and pink covers I have put in a pile in the middle. They find their own and open them, reach for pens and pencils, and wait.

Michelle, who has two children now, one new baby and one two-year-old, does not open her notebook. I do not force her. Once in awhile she does make a list or tries to write a sentence or two. Other days she just listens to others as they read aloud.

All the students in this class are black except Elise, who is white, and Maria, who is Latina. I have been teaching them for the past year, asking them to write instantly on topics and then to read aloud what they have written.

A young woman comes over to me with a registration form in her hand. She is scheduled into a class that meets at this hour across the hall. Since I have gathered young mothers from all over the building for this one hour and Ka Xiong is a young mother, she is joining us for the first time. I smile at her and ask her to sit next to me, take a notebook from the pile of new ones on the shelf behind her.

I could have as many as twelve in this hour but today there are only seven. Some are not in school, others have skipped, a few have stayed in their original rooms to finish up work in order to graduate in a few weeks. Leah and Sheila sit at opposite sides of the table.

WRITING TO UNDERSTAND

who are my protectors?

"Protectors. Who are your protectors?" I ask. "Write a list of them, one or two or ten. Who do you feel you can go to for safety, either emotional or physical safety?"

I begin my own list as they start theirs. I include Maury, my mother, my grown son, my female friends Ruth and Sue, my male friends John and Tom. I put down "police sometimes," firemen, next-door neighbor, brothers, sisters.

I look up as I hear side conversations starting. It has only been a few minutes, but they are all done with this exercise. I ask them to read aloud to me their lists. We go around, one protector at a time, and for a moment the room is filled with the protectors: grandmother Carolyn, Aunt Ruthie, Maria Valdez.

This does not last long. After a few times around the circle they are done. Ka, my new student, does not have one name. I am not sure if she understands the assignment. I ask her if there is anyone in her life she can go to if she needs help.

life w/o ⌢

She shakes her head, says, "I run away. No home no more. Me and my boyfriend and my baby. But my boyfriend not here no more."

The other young women nod their heads. This is a familiar story, sometimes told in standard "White English," sometimes told in African-American dialect, sometimes in Hmong-accented English, like now.

I read the few left on my list. When I mention "police sometimes," the girls snicker.

"Wait a minute. If you are in trouble, you don't ever call the police?" I ask.

"No way. You be in big shit if you do that. And they don't help you no way."

can't call police

Even Sheila nods her head in agreement.

"They just come round an' hassle you, maybe shoot someone, maybe get you in trouble with your friends." Leah says this.

This is a "black thing," someone once told me, this lack of trust in the cops. Today all students agree, including Latina, white, and Hmong.

WRITING TO CAPTURE THEIR VOICES

I ask them to write about one of their protectors in detail: describe a scene with their grandmother, their mother, their auntie, or anyone else who protects them. I tell them to write about a place of safety, a person they can talk to. What does that person look like and sound like? What do they do?

The room becomes silent as they begin. We can hear the cars moving on the street below, the sounds of students in the hallway, the phone ringing in the office down the hall. But right in my room, we concentrate. Even the students who cannot write can usually manage to put down single words that reveal something important about the person, the protector they want to describe. I look at them, their hair in a myriad of styles, some in tiny braids, some in dreads, some close-cropped, some with straightened hair pulled back from foreheads or pulled over to one side. I look at them, with their different-colored skin, from pale white, to blue-black, with coffee and gold, mahogany, red-tinged, and beige in between. I take great comfort in their presence. This is always my favorite time of day. When they begin to read, I know their voices, their words, will be as different as their skin color, their hair. It is the most multicultural, inclusive education I know: to make students' voices the center of the classroom.

I write about my father, how he locked up the house at night, turned off the lights. I write about the time he put his car at the bottom of the road after someone had driven by our house at 80 miles per hour, how he stood at the bottom of the hill and waited for the driver. I describe how he lectured the young man about children, about what would happen to him if he killed a toddler or a young boy on a bike. I can see my dad there, standing in his blue shirt and dark pants, just home from work. I can remember feeling proud of him then, proud of how he stood in the center of our street, protecting us.

After ten minutes I ask them to finish up. Then they begin to read.

Sheila goes first. She has written about her new boyfriend, how he comes over and takes Ayana out once in awhile so she can clean the apartment, rest, read a book.

Leah has written about her mother, who takes care of her child and who buys her things she needs.

Ka says she does not know of anyone right now. She dreams of someone, though.

Toya reads next. She is a young woman who is about to finish up high school. She has read all the black women authors I often recommend, including Toni Morrison, Alice Walker, and Gloria Naylor. Today she has written about her boyfriend, Ken, how they are not together right now since he is in prison, but how she knows when he gets out he will be down for her. She is eight months' pregnant with her first child.

I read aloud what I have written about my father. The room becomes silent for a moment afterward and then Tanya, a light-skinned young woman who is a fine writer, asks if we can write about fathers next. I say sure.

WRITING CLOSE TO THE HEART

"Take ten minutes and write about fathers."

"What if we don't got none around?"

"Write about not having one, then, about what you would like to say to your father if he suddenly appeared in your life. Write your father a letter, if you want."

They bend over their notebooks again. Ka cannot write but sits watching the others. She is so new to us. My hope for her is that she will stay with us long enough to write, talk to our social worker, get advice about her future.

I call time. They look up. Tanya begins the reading. She has written to her father in prison. It is a letter about how much she misses him, about how she knows he loves her and how she will visit him soon. It is not so much her words that touch us all this morning, though. It is her voice, the sadness winding through it there, the ache.

When she is finished, Sheila says, "How come when you read, Tanya, we all want to weep?"

"Girl, you do hit a nerve with me!" says Toya. "Make me wanna go on and leave this sorry school and go home."

"You get Landsman in trouble then. They be sayin' her class made you skip school and then they don't let her teach it no more!"

We laugh. Toya shakes her head and then reads her piece. It is about how when she was little, she had no father at home. She continues, reading to us about being tough since he left them all when she was five, about her mother sometimes being there for her, but since her mother lives in Chicago she can't count on her right now.

How can we be protectors for our students

WRITING TO PLAN FOR THE FUTURE

I have one last topic I want them to think about. There are about twenty minutes left in the hour, so I ask them to write about how they can be protectors for their own children.

Some complain about too much writing, some shake their heads. Some say they will not write. At the same time they reach for their pens. They begin. After about ten minutes I ask them to read again what they have written.

Susan, the one white student in the class, reads about her child, Antonio. She describes how she wants him to live out his dreams because she can never live out her own. She says how she wants to make sure he will be warm and not hungry and how she plans to make sure she talks to his teachers when he gets in trouble.

Leah says she is worried her daughter will get shot. The other young women nod their heads. Many of them here have sons. Out of the six black girls, four have sons. I wonder, fleetingly, as young black men are dying, if these mothers are replacing them.

WRITING TO BUILD RESPECT

We relax into general conversation. Their voices, in here, are respectful. They are so used to taking turns when they read, so used to listening to each other's stories, that they rarely interrupt, even when we simply talk. When we discuss literature, after I read aloud to them, the courtesy extends to these discussions, too.

If we make the thoughts, reactions, and words of our students central to the curriculum, we can have deeper discussions of history, philosophy, science, and

Note

literature. This writing can come through journal entries, in writing a quick response before discussion of a topic, or even in simply noting personal reactions to assignments. There are an infinite number of ways to use writing to make students feel a part of all our classes.

like this [handwritten annotation]

"You worry about your son in New York?" Leah asks me.

"Sure. Just walking home from his restaurant job sometimes, especially when he has cash tips in his pocket. He knows where it is dangerous, and where it's not, though."

"Every place dangerous for us." This from Toya. "Women got to watch out alla time. For they babies and theyselves."

"I hear that, girl," says Tanya. *→ terrible* [handwritten annotation]

"You got to have your man with you, or your friend. You gotta cover your back."

"Not your relatives, though. They ain't gonna help you none." Tanya says this.

"My brother be down for me," says Georgia, a quiet young woman who rarely reads or speaks up in this class. She is scheduled to graduate at the end of the month.

"You lucky, girl."

There is a lull in this conversation.

WRITING TO BRING IN REALITY

I ask them, "So, do you want to go to the bookstore next week? I have the money from the grant. We can pick out books for your kids, and one for you, too."

The girls become unusually silent. Their heads bend toward the table, their fingers fiddle with pencils.

"Naw, Landsman. You bring some books in here. We choose here."

"Come on, " I say, looking around at them. "Let's get out of this building and shop!"

My suggestion dies.

"Okay." I am puzzled. "What's going on here? You usually want to get out of the building."

No sound. Just sullen faces staring out the window, looking at the clock.

"We don't wanna go to no store in Uptown." This from Sheila.

I try to read her face. It is as sullen as the others, giving nothing. I wait.

"You don't get it." This from Leah. "We don't wanna go to no store in Uptown!" She looks directly at me, challenges me to understand.

I do. I get it, finally.

"You get followed." I say this quietly.

They nod their heads.

I could try to reassure them, say I will talk to the clerk, set it all up for them. I could say there will not be many people in there in the morning and that I could make sure all the salespeople will know they are with me. I don't.

"If I could get us a chance to visit an African-American bookstore?" I ask.

They shrug but nod their heads, except for Maria, who is Latina, and Laura, who is white.

"They gonna have any books in Spanish at that African store?" asks Maria.

"I don't know."

"My baby Julio learning Spanish *and* English," she says. "He wanna talk to his grandmother and his daddy."

"You all American now. You gotta learn English anyway." Leah says this without the usual challenge to her tone.

"I want my kids to have two languages. They granpapa's language and they daddy's language."

"Then they be mixed-up kids!" Toya says this, with laughter in her eyes.

Maria laughs. "They mixed up anyway with their father bein' black and all."

"So. We have to get ready for lunch, but I think I will call the African-American bookstore and see if they have Spanish books, too, and some white authors maybe."

Laura nods her head, unconvinced.

"Or maybe I will just go out and get a bunch of books and let you choose here."

There is unanimous agreement that this would be the best idea. Unanimous agreement with their bodies, with the way their shoulders relax, their smiles return. I feel relieved, too, suddenly, and wonder, briefly, if I am taking the easy way out.

I ask them to close up their notebooks, leave them on the table. I will get to these notebooks this week and type up some of what they have written so they can see it "in print" next time.

As they file out, head to lunch, Ka hangs back. She stays in the room after they have all left.

53

"Where did you go to school before now?" I ask.

"Washburn. I left last year though. Just gettin' back in school now after my baby born."

She looks out into the hall but does not leave.

"My brother mad at me. He know I go here now."

"Are you afraid he will come after you?"

She nods her head. "My father tol' him to come get me."

"Let's go talk to someone about this," I say. I lock up the room and we walk down the hall together. When we get to the social worker's office, I go in first, introduce Ka to Ms. Bartholemew, and explain the situation. I leave them then, Liz Bartholemew asking Ka where she lives now, how she gets around the city.

WRITING TO MAKE WOMEN VISIBLE

I go back to my room and pull out a sandwich and a thermos of coffee. My writing class for the women always leaves me feeling as I feel now: Watching the girls on the corner below me flirting with the young men, I am convinced that gender presents a deep and abiding oppression, across all cultures. I feel the complexity of such intersections when I teach young women; the way their sex determines whether they dream certain dreams for themselves, whether they plan to become doctors, lawyers, teachers, geologists, or pilots.

We are getting more and more Hmong and Vietnamese women in our school. They are often on the run, trying to figure out how to live without family any longer. They are caught between the old ways their parents want them to live and the desire they have to go to the mall, date, and hang out with their friends—American style. Their brothers are allowed a great deal more freedom and often take the parents' side in supporting restrictions for their sisters. Some young women in our schools are presently dealing with issues like child brides and female genital mutilation.

I feel an urgency around these things because I see every day what is happening to the lives of the young women who come to my classes. Here at ASP, and at larger high schools across the country, issues around culture, race, and gender come together. Here we are wrestling with a complex interplay of new and old worlds, of rights of women and preservation of culture. The solutions we find and the communication we establish in our city schools can serve the rest of the country in many ways, as our immigrant populations grow and become more and more integrated into the workplaces and communities of the United States.

As I finish this writing class, I see that when my students write and read for each other they become visible to each other, audible to each other. There are times, even if it is just an hour a week, when separate gender classes are worthwhile, when the invisible can be visible, the silent can be heard. It is the hour of the day when I do feel useful, as though Leah and Ka, Sheila and Toya and I are making steps toward solving something bigger than our own individual problems. This class feels large to me, on the edge of important change.

WRITING TO COUNTER ALIENATION

Concerning

Many of us white teachers do not want to confront the truths that come out in these situations. We avoid places and times for discussion, for reading aloud, for journals, for listening. We are nervous about what will be said, what will be directed at us.

Yet it is my firm belief that the alternative to making students the center of the class is to alienate them. Given that white women combined with men and women of color make up over 70 percent of the school population, we are at a risk of losing most of our students altogether if our classes continue to be alienating places. And given the alienation of many young white men from the schools where we teach, it is for our own survival as well as theirs that we need to find ways to make them all part of the dynamics of the class.

I think back to the Hmong child who watched the play with me a week ago. This child was mesmerized to see himself on the stage, in his school auditorium. He laughed with his whole body, was quiet with his whole body. He was transfixed. How many more kids can we mesmerize by simply showing them that we know *they exist?* *Challenge*

The more I teach, the more restless I get in the classroom. I need to change my view, move muscles, talk to other teachers. I need to walk after I eat, even if it is just to the bathroom and back, then to the lunchroom and around the corner to the elevators.

As I head down the hall, Leah stops me.

"I ain't scared of no bookstore, Landsman. We can go if you wanna go."

"I know you aren't scared. I just don't want it to make people tense. It is supposed to be fun."

Leah smiles, a forced smile.

"It be fun. We have a good time, Landsman. I wanna get a book about cars for my son."

"Thanks, Leah. You go ahead and take your break."

She is heading out to the front of the building to smoke. As she turns, I call to her.

"Bad habit, though. Might be nice if you stopped smoking."

"You always be sayin' that, Landsman. Then you tell us about all the students that brought candy to your husband when he quittin'. You bring us candy to quit?"

"If you are really serious."

She smiles, her wide smile that always startles me with its warmth.

"See you, Landsman." She opens the door to the first floor and heads down the stairs. There are about twenty minutes until fourth hour.

It is that exact smile, that sudden honesty and a willingness to risk a trip to the bookstore or a writing exercise that feels scary, that brings me hope. It is the Leahs and the Tyrones, the Sheilas and the Kas who challenge my persistent cynicism. When they are really *with* me, with their words, working all alone on the computer, or when they are speaking honestly, reading out loud all they feel, I sense the power of public education to change this country.

WRITING TO BUCK THE TREND
TOWARD STANDARDIZATION

What does give me pause, however, is that I feel I am bucking a national trend: toward less knowledge of our students themselves, in their entirety and complexity, and more emphasis on content, on prescribed outcomes. Increasingly, I feel I am being asked to adopt a curriculum that comes not from the students and their communities, but from some panel of experts, dictating each hour of our school day, all year long.

I know from experience that each class of students is different from the class I met with the hour before. Each requires a separate preparation and in these classes each student requires some individual attention because

Note

Everyone is different w/ learning

of his or her own unique circumstance or personality. All this can happen if we have classes small enough to get to know our students individually. It *cannot happen* by solely teaching to a test, by prescribed lesson plans, or by mandated curricula.

I am not denying that we need to teach students skills. Yet we do not need to abandon a child-centered approach to do this. We cannot. If we abandon the student in the name of test scores; if we eliminate a celebration of dialect and poetry, in the name of standard English; if we do not combine both skills and creativity, we will lose our students to the streets, to despair, to boredom. So I must hold those voices, the ache as Tanya reads, the way Ka tries to put something down on paper, even during her first day, at the same time that I hear about more regulations, more restrictions on how I teach, what I teach. I persist in my belief that we must do it all: teach skills at the same time we make students' voices an important part of the core of the curriculum.

lose students

However, no one can do it all with 150 students a day. I know this. I also know that it is this class-size situation that often drives good and generous people out of the teaching profession altogether. Teachers are set up to fail. To do our job well, we need to understand how each student learns. I have taught classes of twenty and classes of thirty-five. There is no comparison. The class of twenty learned more, was able to receive more individual help, more diagnostic instruction, than students in the larger classrooms. This is common sense. There is nothing more obvious to teachers and nothing makes us angrier than to be told that class size does not matter. With a complex body of students who read anywhere from first-grade level to college level, with classes full of students who are only beginning to learn English, there is no question that small class sizes make a huge difference in our ability to reach all students.

Last spring, I returned to a middle school where I had taught a year before. When I had taught there, we had twenty-five to thirty students in a class of seventh- and eighth-graders. I never felt I could reach all of them. I found myself frustrated and despairing as they went through my door, the quiet ones giving me a brief wave or smile. When I returned to this school, the class size was reduced to sixteen to eighteen students at a time. The difference was astounding. We could actually fit around the tables assembled all in a row, as though we were at a family dinner together. I spoke to each student, bent over his or her poems, and exchanged jokes and news. The noise level was calmer, the students as serene as seventh- and eighth-graders are capable of being. And I was able to

smaller class sizes

listen to the Hmong girls read from their notebooks, the Ukrainian boy stumble through some of his first words in English. With such classroom numbers the job seemed manageable, the halls quieter, the teachers more relaxed than they had been the year before.

At a time of great teacher shortage, we must look at modifying the working conditions of teachers to make their jobs rewarding and to attract a new and enthusiastic workforce. Drastically lowering class sizes would go a long way toward making a positive change in such conditions. It would change schools into places where skills instruction and creativity could flourish at the same time.

REFLECTION QUESTIONS

1. How can including students' own stories help us to understand them, their lives, their hopes? Why do you think we don't do this more often in schools?
2. Given the emphasis on standardized testing, how can we justify spending time to let students reach into their experiences for essays, stories, poems? Pretend you are addressing a school board and trying to get money for these kinds of programs after school or even during the school day. What would you say to convince them that such activity does ultimately improve student performance?
3. How can we make student voices the center of our classes? In history? In science? In literature?
4. Does using creative writing mean we are abandoning teaching skills like sentence structure, grammar, paragraph and essay construction?

6

LUNCH HOUR

Students' Lives

He could admit personal guilt; he knew what he'd done. Yet if that was all there was to it, why did the world treat him exactly the same when he was doing right, when he had all those jobs and all those stocks and mutual funds? Back then, all his money and standing didn't matter to the sales clerks and security guards, who would follow him around the stores. The world was no different when he drove his Mercedes—bought and paid for with Beth Steel paychecks and tech-stock dividends—and suffered through dozens of police stops and registration checks. Nor did money count when he would get dressed up and bring a date down to the harbor restaurants. His worst, most humiliating memory, was of a cool summer night when he took a girl to City Lights in Harborplace and asked if it might be possible to sit outside on the balcony. No, sorry, he was told; then they were seated at a table by the kitchen while the balcony tables stayed empty for the next two hours. A small insult, of course—nothing that could level a person in a single blow, unless that person came from Fayette Street, where every moment tells you who you are and what you were meant to be.

—Simon and Burns,
The Corner: A Year in the Life of an Inner City Neighborhood

drean

For years I have worried about the separation visible at lunch time in our schools. I have thought that if I could only stand here one day and observe a room full of tables where students mingled, black and white interspersed with Native American and Asian, I would have known we had accomplished some important goals for our country. This always seemed to be the official line, the litmus test of integration. If we integrated the lunchrooms, we would have successfully broken through racial barriers and have arrived in my utopia.

Now, I look in the cafeteria where the kids are eating their lunches. Some of them take quick bites and dance near the tables. Others eat slowly, sit and linger. I like watching them in their time to move or not move, time without teachers and commands for silence. No desks in rows, and no blackboard lists of texts with questions.

I remember once, years ago, being in a balcony at the State Arts High School, watching the mostly white students come from classes to the student lounge where the Clarence Thomas confirmation hearings were being broadcast continuously on television. At first, as the kids came in, they swung knapsacks around onto the chairs, poked each other, laughing, arguing, touching, arms around arms, boy and girl, girl and girl, boy and boy.

Another teacher, John, and I were focused on the hearings as Anita Hill, dignified, in her blue suit, told the men lined up above her about what this candidate for the Supreme Court had done to her.

After about ten minutes, I felt, without looking, that the kids' attention was also riveted on the screen and riveted on her words, her face, eyes, skin, and the sound of her soft voice. John nudged me.

"Look at the kids."

I moved my eyes down to the group. I saw the young girls stiff-backed and quiet, their bodies tucked in, up inside themselves. Their arms, instead of being draped along the backs of sofas, around their boyfriends' shoulders, or under their chins as they studied, were folded over their breasts. They bowed their heads slightly so their hair could cover their cheeks, dip over their eyes. Their faces were tight-muscled, jaws outlined against their skin. Some of them had withdrawn from the boys, from each other, and pulled themselves tight into circles on the big chairs, curled like small children there.

The boys were in their customary poses. They had not changed or shifted that easy slouch, that long-legged awkward sprawl that kids so often as- their jaws and faces were slack with relaxation, even though they and the focused on the same screen.

Learn a lot from watching

"Look at the difference in how they are sitting," John said, and I noticed tears in his eyes. I nodded, that lump of frustration and sorrow building in my throat.

I understood the girls. As I watched, I had felt my own body turn on itself, look to itself for protection. I felt suddenly alone, the way I have felt so many times, finding myself on a walk along the river near my house, cars gone, a man approaching from the opposite direction, no one in sight. Luckily, at the Arts High School, I had just begun a support group for any young woman who wanted to join. We met one evening after school and it seemed to be a place where they could talk openly. Because we had this place, this time, I did not feel totally helpless watching them there, stiff and serious.

Since that day I stop whenever I can, to watch students in places of relaxation, recreation. I do this because I learned more that day about the arrogant-seeming young women I taught in that school, about the young men, and about my male colleague than I had in any number of classes or faculty meetings.

That day as I watched two of my most defiant female students and observed their bodies covered by their own arms, I learned about the similarities that still exist between us as women, about ways, perhaps, to explore this in my classes.

SEPARATION

Now, four years later, I note this about ASP and other high school students in other lunchrooms across the city:

At one set of tables, I see black young men and women. Tyrone is laughing at something another young man is whispering to him. Tanya has finished eating and is leaning back against the table. Her boyfriend is caressing the side of her face with his hand. She is not smiling. One boy is reading a book, while next to him two young men are talking about the CD they hold in their hands. Near them, at another table, a group of young black men are talking animatedly, challenging each other. At a third table of black students, some are playing cards while some watch the game.

At each of these tables, what I notice is the body language, the gesture, the vibration. These young men and women, with mixed hues of black skin, mocha skin, almost-white skin, seem unaware of their bodies in the relaxed way we can be when we are not asked to be other than ourselves. At the moment, they do not seem vigilant. *↳ relax when ourselves*

Near the tables full of black students are two tables where Hmong students sit. They laugh in a slightly more muted way: except for the slim young woman who is arguing with her boyfriend, hands on hips, except for the tall boy who is reading from a book with a mock British accent. Except. Even here I see that generalizations are useless, that the individual actions of my students run counter to every stereotype and even every expectation.

Two young women are lost in books, the way I remember being when I was that age. All around them there are kids talking, pushing, nudging, and they do not move, not a muscle. I cannot see what the books are; I assume they are novels. Maybe because that is how I lost myself.

At another table, two Vietnamese students are arguing with each other. While I can hear, just slightly, their words, I cannot understand them, as they are speaking in their native language. At this same table two other Vietnamese boys are also listening with headsets, lost in music. They move their legs and heads to a beat, insistent, regular. These students are quiet, except for the girl who gets up and dances at the end of the table, singing a rock and roll song and holding a pencil like a microphone. There is also a girl who is arguing with a boy at the next table, hands on hips. Ka is here. She waves to me, then turns back to the table and reaches for a tube of lipstick a friend holds out for her.

Beyond the tables of Hmong students are the white kids. One table has all girls, who are putting on eye shadow, exchanging eyeliner, and glancing over at the table next to them where an all-male group sits, talking and laughing. These girls seem self-conscious, even in this context, slightly stiff or rehearsed. Again, my own experience may be influencing my vision. Unless I was reading a book, I remember being very aware of every move I made in school, even at lunch. My body was of extreme importance then, how it felt when I sat and moved and ate.

Sarah, who has come back to the building and is dressed like the others in tight jeans and a long, tunic sweater with a v-neck, lounges back in her chair. She is reading.

The next table is one of white boys. They are in different poses, and in contrast to the white girls, their bodies seem relaxed. Except for a short boy, with spiky blond hair, who sits stiffly at one end, smiling nervously and eating his lunch slowly. Except for the boy who is gangly and awkward and whose large-wristed hands stick out below his white, soiled shirt. Josh is here, whispering to his neighbor, a bleached blond-haired boy with many rings in his nose and ears and, I am sure, in many places I don't want to imagine right now.

Near the tables for white students are two tables of Native-American students. Some wear their hair long, with headbands. Others have short haircuts, others pull their hair back in ponytails. They are already finishing up their meal and beginning to leave the table, first to go outside for a few minutes before the bell rings. Except three boys who stay and read a book over each other's shoulders.

There are other tables at which sit dark-skinned Somali students newly arrived to this country. They are mostly silent, eyes wandering around the room. The young women are covered in long veils, dresses to their ankles, their faces swathed in fabric.

There is still a part of me that wants all these students to mix more. Such a belief in the necessity for people to intermingle came early in my life. When I was about twenty and home from college, some winter evening during the holiday break, I argued fiercely about this with my father. He paced back and forth across our living room, scotch and water in his hand. Finally, he stopped in front of me. He was freshly showered, out of his work clothes, dressed in ironed khaki pants, a blue and white checked shirt from Brooks Brothers, and a pair of soft leather shoes.

I remember his angry question that evening: "What do you want, Julie? If we go the way you say with all this integration stuff, we will end up a country of 'high yellows'!" I am not sure where he learned this term, a specific skin-color term among blacks, but I could tell from his tone of voice it was not complimentary. ⇐ High yellows

There was a sneer in those last two words. To my father, anyway, "high yellow" meant a disgusting mixture of the races. It was the worst outcome he could imagine for this country.

With the typical defiance of a '60s young woman, I answered, "Yep, that is what I want. A country of 'high yellows.'" My father's blue eyes darkened. He turned away, as if to watch the snow that fell outside across the patio light, his broad back ending our exchange. What seemed then to me a sign of the country's progress was for him a sure sign of its collapse.

At that time I truly thought intermarriage might be the solution to bridging the racial divide. And, in some sense, I still applaud such marriages and feel satisfaction at the increase in kids from mixed cultures in my classroom. I like it, as I have always liked the way some people resist societal restrictions or expectations.

For awhile I decried separatism in any form.

I don't know when I began to change. But now, as I look at the students at their chosen tables, what I see are places of safety. Each group finds, for thirty minutes, a brief respite, a chance to become themselves. Kids who are often nervous, tense, stiff-backed in class, are here relaxing, lounging, jumping.

The first lines of a poem entitled "The Waking" by Theodore Roethke come to me now:

I feel my fate in what I cannot fear.
I learn by going where I have to go.

Perhaps this is where the students have to go. They have to be where they do not have to figure out the white and official world, just for awhile. *They have to be where no one will notice their otherness, because for a brief time, it is not there.* Their bodies tell us how relaxed they are here, insiders on their own territory. After teaching and visiting schools all over the city, I have observed that these different tables are just as noticeable in regular mainstream lunchrooms as in this special site.

In her book *Why Do All the Black Kids Sit Together in the Cafeteria?* Beverly Tatum describes reasons for the students' gathering together at lunch. On pages 53–54 and 60 she gives a rational explanation for what I have observed over the years.

Given the impact of dominant and subordinate status, it is not surprising that researchers have found that adolescents of color are more likely to be actively engaged in an exploration of their racial or ethnic identity than are White adolescents.

Why do Black youths, in particular, think about themselves in terms of race? Because that is how the rest of the world thinks of them. Our self-perceptions are shaped by the messages that we receive from those around us, and when young Black men and women enter adolescence, the racial content of those messages intensifies. . . .

Not only are Black adolescents encountering racism and reflecting on their identity, but their White peers, even when they are not the perpetrators (and sometimes they are), are unprepared to respond in supportive ways. The Black students turn to each other for the much needed support they are not likely to find anywhere else.

And finally, on page 62, she says:

> We need to understand that in racially mixed settings, racial grouping is a developmental process in response to an environmental stressor, racism. Joining with one's peers for support in the face of stress is a positive coping strategy. What is problematic is that the young people are operating with a very limited definition of what it means to be Black, based largely on cultural stereotypes.

The combination of being made aware of their racial identity and encountering racism in adolescence makes it very logical that students of like racial and ethnic groups would want some time to support each other.

The kids throw balled-up napkins into the trash, put away their trays, and head for the hallway or outside to have a quick cigarette before the next class starts. As they leave, they begin to take on, again, like a sweater, a shirt, or a pair of glasses, the stance of the vigilant observer.

For awhile, though, these same students were not preoccupied. For thirty minutes, at lunch, they seemed simply occupied. I wonder why we cannot keep our kids *occupied* like this when we teach. Why, when they come to attention in our classes, they also begin, paradoxically, to let their minds wander, their hands nervously twisting and untwisting locks of hair, turning pencils, tearing up bits of paper.

When I talk to students about this sometimes, on a winter morning in my classroom or after school on the front steps of the building, they usually shrug their shoulders and talk about being bored. Classes seem so irrelevant to the questions and concerns of their lives. They are often worried about a job, a baby, money for their family, or the new CD they want to buy. Rarely do they see what happens outside of school as connected to school itself. And what happens outside of school is often of paramount importance to them. This seems true for so many students today, white or black, middle class or working class.

And if they are students of color, say, they rarely see their own culture reflected in anything they hear or see in school. They tell me that they tune out. That is how they survive. Sometimes, when they are angry at what they are told or at a statement by a teacher, they think about objecting or discussing what they have heard. They are insulted, sometimes, by a condescending tone of voice or a lack of attention to their own history, music, or literature. Yet most of the time, instead of raising a point or asking a question, they give up, submit to the point of view in the room, and leave as soon as possible.

NORMALITY

According to psychologists, adolescents love to be "normal." It is important to them not to stand out. They often want to blend in with others, with their hair, flesh, body shape, clothes, voice, and words. It is hard, then, to begrudge our adolescent students this one half-hour to be where they are not outsiders but rather part of the group.

Often, I hear my colleagues in high schools across the city complaining about how cliquish the students of color are, how they stay to themselves at lunch. I fell into this until a very wise friend pointed out to me that for years white students have chosen to sit in a group, and no one has commented on how cliquish the *whites* are. Cliques of whites based on athletics, economic class, college prep, or vocational track who isolate themselves from each other are seen as *developmentally normal.* When students of color separate themselves, it is termed racial and exclusionary.

The separate tables I see at lunch are part of the natural development of these students and also reflect the separations in our society as a whole. I may not like these separations, I may not approve of the conditions that cause them, but they are there. Students experience them every day on the streets, in stores, and in neighborhoods. So, when I see them happen in the lunchroom it makes sense to me.

Yet I am still torn. As I walk quickly by the tables now empty in the lunchroom, I realize that the kids at those separate tables, the girls who were dancing and the boys who hovered over books, who lounged against the chairs, the ones who quietly brushed aside their hair, have much to learn from *each other,* especially in this informal setting, at lunch.

And more important, perhaps, than this exchange of culture is the fact that at this time, in this country, a certain kind of power resides at those white tables. In large high schools, those blond-haired kids have many of the contacts in the world where money is made. They have more immediate entry into corporate offices, banks, and headquarters. They will inherit entry into the schools where certain vocabularies are spoken, tests taken, knowledge defined: where their fathers, their mothers attended, and those generations before them.

Their lunch tables are like the golf courses where many of the important decisions get made, during those hours when white women are not allowed on the course, and where black men and women are not allowed into the club at all. White males in particular have been receiving affirmative action in these places all along.

To make real equality happen, I know that there will be days when sitting with the white students will be necessary for the students of color. I know that it is in the informal arenas of our life, in the cues and nods, gestures and asides, that so much of the business of the world goes on. Mingling is a good thing once in awhile.

I believe that students of color can keep white students from becoming unduly arrogant. They are important members of the peer group who can stop white students from assuming that their perspective is the single and only truth.

As I see the deserted lunchroom, as I watch who leaves to go to teach, who stays to clean up tables, I see played out before me the divisions and the hierarchies of our country. A Native American man sponges off the chair, while a white woman heads to biology class, lab equipment in her arms. My hope is that once the same kids who dominated this room only a half-hour before have come into power, things may be different.

REFLECTION QUESTIONS

1. What do you remember, or what do you observe today, going on in the hallways, lunchrooms, and outside the doorways of the school you attended or where you work? What can you learn from being in these spaces?

2. Why do you think students sit with their racial or ethnic group in the cafeterias? How important is this? Does the administration or teaching faculty comment on all the white students who are sitting together at their own tables? If not, why not?

3. How can we make our classrooms take into account the fact that many students of color may feel alienated? How can we provide places where we teach that allow for identity development *and* group solidarity?

4. Observe your school carefully. Do people of color dominate the lower paying and more menial positions? What message does this send to students? Also, what message does it send to elementary students that many more teachers in grade schools are women? Why do you think this is the case?

7

FOURTH HOUR

Connections

After the Egyptian and Indian, the Greek and Roman, the Teuton and Mongolian, the Negro is a sort of seventh son, born with a veil, and gifted with second-sight in this American world,—a world which yields him not true self-consciousness, but only lets him see himself through the revelation of the other world. It is a peculiar sensation, this double-consciousness, this sense of always looking at one's self through the eyes of others, *of measuring one's soul by the tape of a world that looks on in amused contempt and pity. One ever feels his two-ness—an American, a negro; two souls, two thoughts, two unreconciled strivings; two warring ideals in one dark body whose dogged strength alone keeps it from being torn asunder.*

The history of the American Negro is the history of this strife—this longing to attain self-consciousness manhood, to merge his double self into a better and truer self. In this merging he wishes neither of the other selves to be lost. He would not Africanize America for America has too much to teach the world and Africa. He would not bleach his Negro soul in a flood of white Americanism, for he knows that Negro blood has a message for the world. He simply wishes to make it possible for

*a man to be both a Negro and an American, without being
cursed and spit upon by his fellows, without having the doors of
Opportunity closed roughly in his face.*

— W. E. B. Du Bois, *The Souls of Black Folk*

I stand at my door, waiting for fourth-hour students to arrive. For a moment they come in unguarded, speaking from their lunchroom stance, from their own communities and languages. As I close the door to my room, I hear Reggie saying something about weed, about some strong stuff, about being "messed up."

"I hope you aren't smoking weed at lunch time, the way some of you do. You get so you can't even concentrate in my class. Just fall asleep."

"You think weed is just dope, huh, Landsman? Just marijuana."

"Yea. Pot," I respond.

"Oh yeah," says Danny, whose long blond hair reaches his shoulders. "She's from the '60s hippie time, when it was only pot. Now it means stronger stuff, like crack, you know, like laced with something."

"You know what a blont is, Landsman?" asks Marcia, a new student who has been observing me all week, since she started coming back to school after six months away.

"Dope rolled like a cigar," I answer. They all smile. Their smiles seem affectionate, as though they are talking to a relative who they believe is trying to "get it" but is a little out of touch. They are pleased I understand what a blont is, as they have been explaining things like this to me all year.

"But strong, like a cigar, Landsman," says David, Marcia's boyfriend, who has dropped into my room for a moment before he goes on to his social studies class.

"You'll be wasted if you smoke blont before you come to class." This from Danny, who watches me carefully. I smile, nod my head.

It is important to know what students are saying. Not just in reference to drugs but in all aspects of their life. When they refer to "bookin," as in "I was bookin as fast as I could"; or "cold," referring to bad, as in "that was cold, man, to do to her"; or "bad," referring to good, as in "he has a bad car, man, leather seats, and all," I need to know what they mean.

These are creative students, and so their language changes all the time. This language is vibrant and innovative. I want such brilliance in my writing classroom. Their language is from their culture and I want that culture in my room.

Trying

At the same time I know this is not my language. I cannot fake it. I don't speak in dialect with them. It is not natural to me to use their words. These terms are not part of my repertoire. What I have found, however, is that students are willing to explain the meaning of new words, the terms for things. They get a kick out of it. They relish my ignorance of the vocabulary of their day-to-day exchange. They are in power here, I am the one who has to ask for information. They are letting me in on their lives, their intimate language, how they live after school. I never cease to be amazed at their patience.

"Okay now, let's get going. Some of you need to get your autobiographies done soon. So you can graduate."

They come to the front of the room, grab their disks, and settle at desks, talking to each other. David whispers in Marcia's ear before he leaves the room. He touches her neck. She laughs, then pushes him away. I am waiting for Preston. He is late.

In five minutes everyone is quiet, tapping away at computers. I move around, suggesting changes, revisions. Preston walks in the door, earphones from his Walkman around his neck, the cord reaching to his coat pocket. Preston is a square young man, dark-skinned and solid. He is about six feet tall, wearing baggy pants, a starter jacket, and a beautiful blue dress shirt. Some days he comes in sweats. On days like this he comes in looking as though he is headed for a job interview. Preston told me once about a gun that he kept in the glove compartment of his car when he was driving to Illinois. He kept it for the part where he drove for the miles through "white country" before he arrived at his mother's apartment in the Robert Taylor Homes. _Sad_

Preston was recently in prison for six months, because cops found drugs in his apartment one week last summer. He has told me the whole thing was a set-up, that there were people staying with him from Chicago, and he didn't know they were dealing.

"But since they found the stuff in my crib, well, you know, Landsman," he said, shrugging his shoulders. "Jus' the way it go, you know."

I walk up to my desk, where he is standing. I ask him what he is working on now, suggest he take his disk and get started. Preston has his own corner of the room, with the same computer he uses each day. No one messes with Preston's spot. Now he smiles, leans on my desk.

"Landsman, you think I can go to Jones room and work on my SAT practice? I got to take those tests in two weeks, man, and she got the whole practice disk in there."

"So, you are still going to take the SATs in June?"

"Yeah, man, I got to do good on them for after this place."

Preston wants to go on to college, is determined to make his money in the "white world" now.

"Are you going to do the English part then? Since this is English class?"

Preston ducks his head and looks up again, smiles. When he smiles, I do, too. It is instinctive when I am with Preston to respond to him by smiling back. I have seen him work this magic on others. He is charming and smart.

"Aww, Landsman. I do fine on the practice stuff for English. I jus' need to learn how to *think* a certain way for my math." This is true. Preston's English and vocabulary skills are excellent.

"Is Jones in the room?"

"Yeah. She there. I saw her when I went by."

I let him go. As I am heading for the phone to call Jones, Marcia calls me over to look at her computer: the paper feeder seems to be jammed. There is nothing that frustrates students more than having a mechanical mishap with the machines in this computer English room. I help Marcia line up the paper and we print off her story.

Reggie asks, "Can I open the windows? It's gettin funky in here."

"I hear that," says Danny, looking up.

Marcia, who has now gotten up to find a book to read, says, "Who you callin' funky, boy?" She is smiling at Reggie.

"Not you, baby, definitely not you," he says. He walks over to her and stands in front of her, his body close. She puts her hands on his shoulders and pushes him backward. He staggers a moment, straightens up, shakes his head, and walks over and pulls at the large windows, letting in a weak May breeze. Then he goes back to his desk. Marcia takes a science fiction novel from my shelf and heads back to her desk.

GIVING STUDENTS MANY CHANCES

Finally, they are all settled down, working. It is sleepy, with even the sound of the cars muted on the street below, redolent, humming. Once in awhile their radios send out quick rap beats, loud news voices as they speed by. I begin to write up the attendance sheet for the hour.

The phone rings. It is Susan Jones.

"Did you know that Preston was here?"

"Oh. I was on my way to call you five minutes ago. I'm sorry. The paper jammed."

"Well. This is his English hour and he is supposed to be working on that, not math."

I can hear Preston behind her. He is angry. If there is one thing I have not wanted to experience, it is Preston truly worked up. He is muttering something about "Forget it."

"I know, Susan. He just wanted to work on his math skills before the SATs in a few weeks. I thought, maybe just this once, he could spend an hour in there."

"Well, I don't want him now."

I hang up the phone. Even though I have not gotten along with this woman very well this year, I am still surprised by the anger in her voice. Preston comes storming in less than a minute later.

"Damn, Landsman, she start talkin' about me doin' math 'stead of English, because this is my English hour. Man!"

Before I can say anything else, Susan Jones comes in. She is a tall woman with hair pulled back behind her ears. Susan is about forty-five years old and has been teaching students like Preston for at least fifteen years. She looks at him now as he stands at my desk, glaring at her.

"This is his English hour, not his math hour. What are you doing letting him work on math during his English hour?"

"See Landsman, she crazy!" Preston says, shaking his head.

"Preston, go sit down. Just take your usual seat."

"She makin' me mad, Landsman. Shit." He shakes his head again. He is hesitating between the door and his seat in the corner.

"Please, Preston. Sit down back there for a while."

"Let's go out into the hall," I say to Susan.

"Fine," she says. We walk out the door together. The rest of my students are silent. Preston is back in his corner, his earphones on his head. He is staring down at the floor.

"Look. I should have called you. He only needed today to study for the test. It is unusual that I let my students go."

She turns from me and starts down to her room.

"Send him if you want then," she says, conceding without apologizing. "But I have to do some stuff in the office since my students are gone on that field trip. So I won't be there to help him." She keeps going, marching; her chin juts forward.

I know she is a good teacher. I know she can teach math and I know that students can learn from her. Yet today I sense a hostility in her toward both Preston and me that I cannot explain. I know I have had bad days. I hope I have not treated another teacher like this in front of students. I hope I have not lost my belief in a student no matter how many times he or she has let me down. This is hard. I wonder if perhaps I have given up on someone in more subtle ways. We are not superhuman here.

When I get back to the room, Reggie says to me, "Man. She dogged your ass."

Preston takes off his earphones. He comes up to my desk. "What she say?"

"She said you can go on back down and work on the computer, but she won't be there because she has to go to the office."

"Awww shit, man. I can't stay in that room, nobody there. If anything was stolen, they could say it was me. I can't be all alone in a room with all that equipment. Shit!"

I am surprised.

"Yup." This from Reggie, who has not gotten to work. The rest of the students are back on their computers. Once they begin writing, they often get lost in their words. I have always felt that the individual computers create a kind of private space around them and that they feel alone when they sit there, especially if they wear earphones and listen to music. I often write with music playing. I think this may help them get their words out.

"Just go on down there, Preston. Work on your math stuff." He shakes his head.

Preston deserves another chance. I believe many students I teach deserve many chances. However, I feel more and more that I am isolated in this belief. This isolation stems from the fact that I want eighteen- and twenty-one-year-old young men and women I teach to have the chance to start over, despite prison and drug dealing, despite suspensions and expulsions from schools, despite bad language, despite mistakes. I want them to have more than three strikes. In many ways I want them to be able to start over every day they come in the door of our schools.

I want this for them because I have seen them turn around year after year. I have been teaching long enough to know my faith in them is very often justified. I believe Susan, although she is angry today, wants the same thing for students like Preston. Many of my friends in this school and in this city want it. Yet we feel in a minority these days.

UNDERSTANDING VIGILANCE

Preston looks at me. "I can't be alone in that room, Landsman, I just can't. Something might be taken already and then they say I did it." He walks back to his desk and gets out a book I have given him to read. He opens it. I can tell by the way his foot taps on the floor that he is not really reading. He has caught me slightly off-guard. I had not thought of this angle to his situation.

This is Preston, then—black in a white world, trained to distrust us whom he has observed distrust him. He has seen, has experienced false accusations. His is an educated caution. All our talk, all our teaching, then, with Preston and his brothers and sisters is accompanied by this caution: his knowledge of what we *might* do. No matter what I say, I will not be able to, and, in a sense, I *should not*, relax this tension in him. *disappointing*

And, too, this kind of vigilance is what you have if you are Sheila. You must never find yourself alone where you might be accused of taking jewelry out of someone's purse, money from a wallet, even though you would never think of doing this, even if your mother has raised you not to steal.

You have learned, most of the time all on your own, to leave when you cannot control what might happen. You are surrounded by people like those who have accused you first and accused that little white-skinned thief you saw snitch the lipstick, later. Sheila and I have talked about this, on mornings when she comes in after being followed, on days when she is the most exhausted.

I am not naïve enough to think that black students never steal or that Preston's past does not figure into a teacher's caution around him. Yet I know that many African-American friends who are middle class, who are college-educated with no record at all, live in the same vigilant way these students live. I know I have never had to maintain such caution. *no record*

I have never had to be on guard in this way, looking in the rearview mirror of my life to see what is coming from behind: what might pass me and show up in my future. The closest I can come to such a stance is the caution I feel because I am a woman, the times when I have to anticipate the early winter darkness, the walk to my car, the chance of danger. Yet such a situation is clear, obvious to me. On most days, going about my shopping, my appointments, I do not have to think four and five steps ahead, anticipate accusation, rebuff, or refusal. I do not have to plan my life around the *possibilities* of situations leading to other situations. *Don't know*

shouldn't have to

All their lives the mothers and fathers, the sisters and brothers of the students in our classrooms have _necessarily_ trained them to beware of many dangers that we whites do not see and that the white world creates for them.

ACKNOWLEDGING STUDENTS' PERCEPTIONS OF THE WORLD

Inspiring

The least I can do is acknowledge the perceptions of the world that students bring to me: perceptions about the difference their skin color makes in the way they are considered by store owners, teachers, policemen, and bosses. This does not mean I have to excuse students for behavior that is hurtful or treat them as though they are victims. It does not mean I have to change what I expect of them.

It does mean I have to believe what they tell me about their lives, the way they might be accused, the experiences they have out on the street. I cannot deny their perception of the world. Rather, I have to start with an understanding of this perception, go on from it and plan with them how they will study, make it in college, stay on the job.

FINDING MENTORS FROM THE STUDENTS' COMMUNITY

I glance up at the clock. I tell Reggie, Preston, David, and Marcia that they can get ready to go. They stay focused on their screens for a while longer, then gradually bring up their disks to the holder at the front of the room and go to stand by the door. Alan, the aide in my room for the next few hours, has come in to get ready to work with me.

"Where were you this morning, man?" asks Reggie. "Nobody unlocked the pop machine. You 'sposed to be doin' that, ain't you?"

"My car broke down last night," Alan smiles.

"Not surprised, that funky ol' car you got. Some Toyota thing like that, man."

"Where you break down?"

"Over in Kenwood. Midnight."

"What goin' on, man? You got some fine Kenwood woman, huh?"

"No. I was taking a different way home. Wanted to avoid some accident."

"What you do?"

"Pull over. Put the hood up. Then I see the lights go on in the houses, see people peeking out of their windows. I wait for the cops."

The black kids laugh. "Ain't that right, man. You know the cops gonna be there."

"So, they come, man?"

"Yeah. You know. Hands up, the search, stuff like that."

"How you stand that?"

"I jus' tell them where I work. I just keep saying it over and over. You know: name, address, place of employment."

These young men, at least half of whom have been in jail for minor offenses, listen carefully as he says, "I just say, 'I am Alan Jones. I live at 1854 Lyndale Avenue. I work at Academic Support Program. I also work at Glen Lake. My phone number is 725-1557. My name is Alan Jones. I live at 1854 Lyndale Avenue. I work at Academic Support Program. I also work at Glen Lake. My phone number is 725-1557.'" *B. Learned*

"Yeah, man, we know. You Alan Jones. We know. How long you say it?"

"I keep saying it until the cops calm down."

I have heard this story before from Alan. Yet what I notice now, as Alan is telling students about what happened, is the utter silence in the room. Usually these young men and women are kidding each other at the end of class, pushing each other out into the hallway, laughing. Now they are quiet, concentrating.

It is time to go. On most days they would be out the door. Now they stay, not noticing the clock.

Preston asks the question they all have on their minds. They nod their heads when he says: "But man, what do you do about feelin' mad and all? I mean what do you do when they talk about you 'nigger this and nigger that'? How do you keep from going off, man?"

Alan replies: "I just keep saying the words about myself over and over so I don't really hear what they're saying."

"I don't know," one young man says. "Seems like to me it is your respect you got to give up. Don't know if I can do that."

"Or your life," says Alan. "Your respect or your life. You take your chances if you back talk a cop."

They walk out slowly, puzzling, shaking their heads. Alan has brought into the class his way of dealing with something they deal with every week. He has shown them not only the vigilance he keeps, but the tactics he uses when something happens despite his vigilance. He is taking them a step further.

Alan's experience is invaluable. He is the kind of man who should be in our schools all the time, all day long: be it in the role of counselor, principal, teacher, aide, secretary, social worker, or psychologist. We need men and women of color who can talk about their lives, bring their stories into the room, the way students bring theirs.

I saw these students listen with this intensity one other time this year. Again, it involved Alan. That day Jamal, new to ASP, handed Alan a disk for his computer and said, "There you go, pimp. There's the disk. You wanna file it for me?"

Alan stopped Jamal cold. He raised his voice to a level where he knew the others, bent over their own computers, could hear him, and he said, "You don't call me pimp. And I am going to tell you why you don't call me pimp: because pimps don't work for a living. And you see me here every day working, don't you? I go onto a class afterwards and a night job. So don't call me pimp. The other things pimps don't do: they don't respect women. And I respect women. So don't go calling me pimp."

Jamal shook his head. He grabbed his disk and filed it under his name and went back to where all the other students were now sitting, their eyes on Alan.

Jamal muttered to them, loud enough so Alan could hear, "What a sorry mother. You see the way he treated me, man?"

Before Alan or I could step in, talk about the language that was not allowed in my classroom, another student, Marlin, sitting at a computer, a few weeks away from graduating, looked at Jamal.

"Just listen to him, man. Just listen to him. He teach you things." The rest nodded their heads, went back to the screens in front of them.

Jamal shrugged his shoulders and stared out the window. Yet he had heard what his peers were saying, took in the way they nodded their heads. The next day he got to work, and for a month after that, until he disappeared, he did not challenge either Alan or myself.

There are many times that we, as white teachers, cannot reach certain students the way someone of their own skin color or culture can reach them. I have watched Alan and other black adult men over the years talk with these students about their lives. These students know Alan understands them. Like them, he is stopped and questioned by cops, bureaucrats, shop owners, hotel managers, and waiters all the time. I am not saying that Alan is accepted or even taken seriously by every student in this school. Some of the young men write him off as too white, or too uptight, just as they write off some students for the same reasons. However, even those young men hear what he is saying and take in his suggestions without acknowledging his expertise. I believe his experiences as a black man enable his words to get through at a deep, almost unconscious level, even with the toughest students at ASP. Unlike some of the young black men in this school, I believe Alan has confidence that he can keep up his day-to-day life of shopping, driving, eating in restaurants, and going to bookstores, without having anger dominate his every action. It is important for all students to see and hear this about him.

Of course, he should not have to put up with being harassed. Of course, neither he nor the students with whom I work should have to choose between their self-respect and their survival. At the same time, Alan experiences the world as it is now, today, in this United States, and the students who listen to him know he knows.

We need, then, the visitors—the David Haynes, the writers, artists, the speakers—in our schools all the time. We also need more permanent men and women of color in our buildings. It is the day-to-day contact with Alan that has greatly influenced some of the young men I see come through my door. It is talking to him about his classes at Metro State or watching him teach and noting his presence, on a consistent basis, month after month, that has changed the lives of some of my students. They absorb his black skin and his success in this one man they see before them each afternoon. I, too, have learned from Alan, more than I even know. He has shown me by his persistence in demanding the most from these young men and women who have the same skin color as himself that I must continue to demand this, too. I can be a pushover at times: let a paper slide by, ignore a comment that is negative, excuse a student from class who has missed a lot of school already. Alan calls me on this.

And, too, he has allowed me to see on days like this the absolute power of his presence. I paid lip service to this before, believed it on an intellectual level. Now I believe it in my heart.

Classes are passing. I stand with Alan at the door as some of the students leave. Some, like Reggie, stay with me for another hour.

"Good talk with those guys."

Alan smiles. "Yeah. We'll see, though."

REFLECTION QUESTIONS

1. Put Du Bois's term "double consciousness" in the epigraph to this chapter into your own words. What might it mean to live as though you are being observed all the time instead of simply "being"? If you are not white in this country, how do you describe this? Have you felt this or not?
2. Do you think teachers are willing to give students many chances to succeed? When developmental psychologists tell you that much of a child's potential is determined by the time a child is three or four, do you believe this? What does it imply for education?
3. What does it mean to be vigilant in this chapter? What does this mean for you as a teacher? As a coworker?
4. Think of some mentors, speakers, tutors who might come to your community school. How can they be integrated into the building and into the curriculum? Could you build year round this idea of bringing in the community artists, professionals, and activists? What could you do to make this happen?

8

INTERLUDE

Twenty-Four Seven

It is a sleepy time of day. Some of the kids have left for the afternoon. Others are walking slowly to class. The rooms are warm now. I pull down the shades that cover all the windows. Reggie is sitting in his chair, leaning back.

"Hey, Alan, man," he calls out as Alan walks over to the desk and looks at the class roster for fifth hour. Alan often takes the first few minutes to go outside and round up students who are smoking in front of the building.

"I got my first DWB las' week. Only been drivin' about a month." Both of them smile, as do many of the other young black men who are drifting in.

"Shit, I got mine on the first day I went out. Throwed me up against the side of the squad, searched me, said I looked like someone stole some money from a lady five miles away." This from Tyrone, who is back to do some work on his final autobiography. When I first heard these initials, I didn't get it. Tyrone explained it to me at the beginning of this year. DWB means *Driving While Black*.

I have heard of it since from Alan and from my husband's students and colleagues at the law school, no matter their suits and ties or their fine trucks or cars. To deny that this happens is to deny the everyday truth of our students' and our colleagues' lives.

As I watch them settle down, joke with each other a little more about driving while black, I am aware again of how I am received in the world as a white person. I do not have to first clear the obstacle of a frown, the lack of reciprocation to an outstretched hand, the tiny flutter of refusal before an arm is put forward.

Such hostility is wearying. I have felt it once in awhile at a new job or in a new classroom of students or adults. At times I have felt it when I am teaching groups of young men and I bring up sexism. They bristle or turn away, and later, after class, they do not come up to talk. They accuse me of having a *point of view*, of not being *neutral* like they are. It has always been interesting to me how some white men claim the ability to be neutral, attributing to all others "points of view."

But I do not live with this every day. Challenges to my trustworthiness, to my accuracy, to my credibility are the exception.

If I saw and felt suspicion each day, or even weekly, I believe I might want my own neighborhood. I might want whole blocks that were filled with those who, because of a similar skin color, would not necessarily make judgments about me before I began to live among them. I might want stores and salons, bars and restaurants that were filled with people who would carry cosmetics for my skin color, who would know how to cut my hair, who would warm to my smile, immediately, who would not ask for my ID over and over.

REFLECTION QUESTIONS

1. What happens during racial profiling? Has this happened to you or anyone you know?
2. If people build whole suburbs to keep people out whom they don't like, whether it be according to class or race, does it then make any sense that those of color, or of the same culture, might want to do that themselves? What role can schools play to reach across these identity impulses and groupings?

9

FIFTH HOUR

Representing

And all of this while a steady procession of black faces passed before your eyes, the round faces of babies and the chipped, worn faces of the old; beautiful faces that made me understand the transformation that Asante and other black Americans claimed to have undergone after their first visit to freedom that comes from not feeling watched, the freedom of believing that your hair grows as it's supposed to grow and that your rump sways the way a rump is supposed to sway. You could see a man talking to himself as just plain crazy, or read about the criminal on the front page of the daily paper and ponder the corruption of the human heart, without having to think about whether the criminal or lunatic said something about your own fate. Here the world was black, and so you were just you; you could discover all those things that were unique to your life without living a lie or committing betrayal.

—Barack Obama, *Dreams from My Father*

As she comes in the door, Tameka recites perfectly, musically, Gwendolyn Brooks's poem: "To Those of My Sisters Who Kept Their Naturals." Sarah comes behind her, just as she promised, back for fifth hour. She joins in on the last lines: "Sisters!/ Your hair is Celebration in the World!"

Sarah dips her head down and flings back her curly blond hair, letting it fall wild and tangled around her face.

Tameka laughs. "This is a poem for *my* hair!" She pulls at her dreads, lets them bounce back against her face.

Sarah pulls at her curls, lets them bounce back.

"Go on, girlfriend," says Tameka, brushing her off. "Go on and forget that ol' hair."

They slap palms, sit down opposite each other at computers. I bring them their disks. Josh comes in now. He tells me his art teacher said he could come down here and work on his story. I nod my head, call his teacher to verify, and signal him to sit down. Ka stands before me, shifting from foot to foot. This is her English hour so I get out a new disk for her and set her up at her computer. She must go through a short tutorial on how to use these antiquated computers before she can start on her story. She is impatient to write. She pushes the buttons to move fast through the instructions.

"You already know this stuff?" I ask.

"Yes. I learn it at my old school."

"Okay. Let's start you on the first contract." I get a new disk and put her name on it with magic marker. I hand her a contract, one where she will be answering questions from her own point of view, taking sides, stating opinions.

"I want to write my autobiography. I want to write those things we wrote this morning."

This is a more advanced contract. I look at her, her face turned up toward me. I find the Creative Writing contract and give it to her. One of the things I love about working in alternative schools is that we get to do this. We get to change the order of things, the rules. This is how we sometimes keep students coming to class with us who have dropped out of traditional schools.

Like this

"If it gets too difficult or confusing, just come find me."

She smiles for the first time.

Reggie is standing next to me. He has been waiting patiently there for the last few minutes while I have set up Ka with her work.

"You are supposed to be in math, Reggie."

"Naw, man, I got permission from Jones."

"Let me check." All I need is another misunderstanding with Susan. She tells me she did not give Reggie permission to come down to my room.

"Sorry, Reg. Jones wants you there to do your math."

"Aw, man. Why I gotta go there?"

"Yeah, Landsman, why he gotta go there? He need to do his English." This is from Sarah.

Tameka chimes in, "He need all the help he can get, Landsman. Let him stay."

"I can't, Reg. I can't do that."

"Shit. I ain' goin then. I'll just skip out this mother fuckin' school. Shit!" He sits down hard in his chair.

"Watch the language," Alan says from across the room.

I believe that Reg does not want to stay in this class for me or to make up credits in English. He wants to stay in it because there are some interesting young women here. He has not even gone to get his disk out of the holder or started his work.

Alan walks over to Reggie. He leans down next to him. Reg folds his arms across his chest. I begin working with Tameka, getting her started on her essay on violence. She peeks under my arm to watch the interaction between Alan and Reggie.

"Come on, man. You got to get to that math class."

Reggie leans his elbows on his knees, his chin in his hands. He stares out the window.

Ka has her hand up. I ask Tameka to get to work and to ignore Reggie. Sure, I know this is almost impossible. The scene with him is fascinating.

I lean over Ka. She is saying so quietly that I have to bend down close to her mouth, "My family's trip. I wanna write about my family trip here on the plane."

"Fine. Start there. Make this your American journey autobiography."

"American journey autobiography," she says and begins, counting on her fingers back to four years ago when she arrived in New York. She writes in the date, "August, 1996."

Alan is still talking to Reg. Tameka, clearly listening, is ready to jump in with her thoughts.

"Man. I can work here. I'm two years behind. I got plenty of English I need! I should have two hours in here anyway."

"Doesn't matter. You've got a math class scheduled. You need to get there."

"I don't care about no fuckin' schedule."

"Hey." Alan holds up a hand. "I told you, man, watch how you are talking."

"Sorry, man. I jus' wanna stay in here."

Since I do not have a lot of students in this hour, I have another idea.

"Why don't you go to the office and see if they can change around some of your classes? Then you could be here two hours a day and get a math class another hour."

"You go with me?" Reg looks at Alan. Alan looks at me. I nod.

"Fine. I will just walk him down there. Be right back."

Reggie gets reluctantly to his feet just as Nancy comes in. Nancy is a young woman who wears the head covering that many of my female African-American students wear. She once told me that she is not a religious Muslim. As a matter of fact, she is not a Muslim at all. She and a number of her friends have decided to wear the head covering because they noticed that the boys do not hassle their Muslim classmates so much, but rather treated them with respect.

sad

"Keep me out of trouble," she has told me, smiling.

"Hey girl!" Tameka greets her. "You havin' another of your parties this weekend, huh?"

"Yeah. Down at the Radisson Hotel. Five dollars get you in. S'all."

I walk over to Tameka. She looks at me. "I know, Landsman. I got to get to work, right?"

"You got that. You all set there?" I notice she has her disk booted up and her essay started.

"Yeah. I be fine here." Tameka squints at the screen.

"Hey. You gonna do that job stuff today?" This from Sarah.

"If you all get some work done, we'll start the interview stuff. In fifteen minutes."

Sarah goes back to her work. She is referring to a discussion I have with students once in awhile. I post an article under the title "Issue of the Week" on a board. Lately, they have wanted to talk about work and careers. So we have been discussing applications, essays, interviewing, and other issues that might come up on the job itself.

Tyrone walks in. He grabs his disk and sits down.

"Got me a new apartment, I think," he smiles. "Got to go over there this afternoon before I go to work."

"Hey, Ty, you goin' to Nancy's party?" Tameka asks. Tameka can be distracted easily.

"Oh girl, you havin' one of them parties?" Tyrone goes over to where Nancy is starting on her work.

"Yeah, I am. You comin'?"

"I comin'. You know I don't miss your ol' parties, girl." He smiles. He walks over to her, gives her a hug, one arm around her shoulders. Nancy is one of those quiet kids who somehow slipped through the cracks. She hated junior high school. She rarely attended. She was passed along to high school. Her parents kept moving around the city because they lost their housing or were evicted. She was rarely in one school more than a few months. Now she has found ASP and seems to like it. She may graduate next June if she just keeps coming.

I have often wondered about her parties. From what the students tell me, Nancy sets up "no guns, no liquor" parties at a hotel downtown about once every other month. Everyone is welcome who will follow the rules. The hotel keeps a cut of the take at the door and it is understood that if there is any trouble, the parties will stop for good.

"Gang bangers come, check their guns in the bushes before they come in," Sarah told me during one of our after-school discussions.

"Don't know why it works for her," she said, after I asked her how Nancy is able to organize this so well.

"Guess people jus' wanna boogie without no mess," she said, smiling. "You know what I mean by 'boogie,' Landsman?" She was laughing.

Now Sarah is intent on her work. The pale skin on her neck shows when she bends her head over a book she is reading to gather quotes. Again, I am amazed at how she can pull it off: her immaculate shirt, her clean hair. But then, I am amazed at Tyrone's ability to change apartments, work at his mail-sorting job, get to the novels he wants to read, and find time for parties.

Alan comes back. Reggie is not with him.

"What happened?" asks Tameka, ever vigilant to the comings and goings from the room. "Where Reggie at, man?"

"He is still getting his schedule worked out. He's got to go on his old one for a day to get it all changed."

"That's dog, man." Tameka turns back to her work.

Leah comes in. She has art this hour, and I have an agreement with her teacher that she and Josh can come down if they finish their projects. She has a pass, and so I put her on her own computer.

We are settled in. For fifteen minutes I leave them to their work. I drift around, give them ideas about what to write, how to revise. I check their work.

What I see in this room, right now, are their *differences,* one from the other. Nancy is quiet, Leah is already talking to Sarah, Sarah wants to go back to her novel. Tyrone is intent on his autobiography and no one messes with him, and Tameka is getting out her purse to put on lipstick. I see them as different: not different as black from white, but student from student. Every time I notice this, I become conscious of the absurdity of asking that any of them "represent" anyone but themselves.

And it is exactly the phenomenon of representation that has made me feel real hesitation in writing this book at all. The hesitation comes from my fear that my students will be seen as representatives of *all* black kids, *all* street girls, *all* Asian students, when they are their own unique and complicated selves.

I heard a story from a teacher across the city, who taught in a primarily African-American section of Minneapolis. After the verdict in the criminal O. J. Simpson trial was announced, cameras were all over the school. One reporter leaped out at a young African-American student carrying books out to the car for his teacher. She asked this seventeen-year-old about his reaction to O. J.'s winning—what it meant to him as a young black man, how he felt about it.

He said he did not want to talk about it. She backed off. But when he started up toward his next class, she was there again with her cameraman, her lights, and her insistent voice. Again he walked by her. This teacher asked him what he would have said if he had decided to respond to her question.

"I would have asked her if all them cameras went out to *white* schools in the suburbs and talked to young white men when that Kennedy man's nephew got acquitted of rape. Did she want to know then how *white* men feel about a *white* man getting off?"

This young man's question was never asked. And I wish it had been because he had found a powerful analogy. His analogy had demonstrated how absurd it is to insist that people of color speak for every one of their race. He had also shown, by the absurdity of this question, how whites are considered the norm, so are asked to speak only for themselves *as individuals.* We need only act for ourselves *as individuals.* We assume we do wrong *as individuals.* Meanwhile, blacks are often expected to speak for or represent all blacks.

It happens on subways as a middle-class black family sits near boisterous black kids playing music too loudly. In the eyes of many whites on the subway, the black family is somehow linked with the young black men. This family is silently being asked to talk to "their people," shut them up. I know because I catch myself feeling this way sometimes.

It happens when white people talk about "black people having to get it together" and stop all those blacks from killing each other . . . as though the black doctor in Cincinnati is responsible for the black kid in the Bronx merely because they have the same color skin. It happens inside the minds of black friends who cringe every time a murder is committed, hoping the murderer is not black and that they will not be asked to explain his or her act.

I do not have to explain what other white people do. I even find myself feeling relieved when a rapist, a shoplifter, or a murderer is white. Because then no one else will be "represented by" this individual. He will just be considered to be acting in the complicated evil way that human beings can act, given the mornings and evenings of their lives.

The problem is compounded by statistics and news reports that claim to show "black peoples'" responses to the O. J. verdict by showing videotape taken at one women's shelter in one city. After years of getting to know students, after talking with them each day and working with them in the classroom for years, I am convinced that statistics simply cannot tell me anything about an individual act. And while other groups may be asked to speak for their entire religion, their culture, I am convinced it is not as pervasive, as constant, as it is for African Americans in this country.

TAKING AWAY THE BURDEN:
RESPECTING INDIVIDUAL LIVES

I have learned that if a child is regularly beaten, spanked, or hit during his earliest years, he carries this with him forever. I have learned that the interweaving of poverty and geography, cold streets and houses and no heating oil, can have different effects on our bodies that last and influence who we are, later; that what class we are born into influences the rest of our lives.

As I grow older, I am more and more aware of the way we are separated by our own pattern of nerves, by the cold or the hills where we grew up, by the way the stone walls curved around our years. I am aware of the way some of us were raised with the mountains behind us as we went to school, and how this might have an effect on our lives. To ask any one of us to speak for a group, to award anyone responsibility for his or her entire race or to exact penalty for a whole group based on an individual action is against all I am learning is true of our finely tuned and complex individual lives. *Important*

TAKING AWAY THE ABSURDITY: WATCHING FOR "THE ONLY"

More and more in our suburban schools, black, Native American, or Asian students are the "only one" in their classes: the only person of color in the room. Black students are frequently asked about slavery in the United States as though they are the experts, the representatives of the "black reaction" to slavery. Rarely are white students even asked about slavery from a "white perspective," from the perspective of coming to grips with the phenomenon of whites owning other human beings and what that might mean to them.

The classroom is a public place. In its most hierarchical, it has one leader and an audience of listeners. Once in awhile those listeners are asked to express an opinion. If I must represent anyone else when I speak in this public context, then I might as well keep silent. But silence, in this case, is not my agreement with what is being said. Rather, silence is my protection, my relief, my escape from the absurdity of being asked to represent an entire race. This is especially true if I am, say, the only black student in a class of white students. *Silence*

I find I must be vigilant with myself. I watch for an unmediated reaction, my tendency to assume a young person of color is "typical" of his or her cultural group. I had heard a lot about Somali men when many Somali immigrants came to Minneapolis. I was told these men were sexist and arrogant, that the veiled women were downtrodden. I took in this stereotype and it became part of my perception. Gradually, after more and more contact with young men and women from this culture, I have begun to lose my generalized response, my stereotyped reactions. I feel there are many aspects to the way women are treated and perceived in Somali culture: some I speak out against, some I accept. I have found Somali men who join me in a concern for the liberation of their daughters. I find strong Somali women who are now lawyers, trying to change some customs that have kept women down. I am retraining my mind, again. I am beginning to see individuals where I had let myself perceive generalized groups.

Sheila is Sheila. She does not represent "teenage mothers" or "African-American" teenagers. Just as Sarah is herself: a model, a novel reader, a homeless young woman; so Sheila is herself: a whiz at computers, a good writer, a mother of one daughter. This is how I struggle to see them, to see every part of them. It takes patience with ourselves to get rid of the impulses we were brought up to feel. I believe it can be done.

*See every part *

REFLECTION QUESTIONS

1. What does Barack Obama mean in the epigraph when he says "You were just you"?
2. Gloria Ladson-Billings says that being a culturally competent teacher is a "state of being." What do you think she means by this?
3. In order to counter our impulse to see people of color as representing their entire group, what can we do in school classrooms? On the job? How can we make students critical of the media, of those who demand this representation from individuals of color? What can we do personally when this comes up with groups of friends or colleagues? Is this our own kind of white vigilance if we are white?
4. Why do you think white people are uncomfortable with discussions about these issues? Is there fear or guilt connected with this?

10

MY WHITE
POWER WORLD

But parents who don't function within that culture [of power]
often want something else. . . . They want to ensure that the
school provides their children with discourse patterns, interac-
tional styles, and spoken and written language codes that will
allow them success in the larger society.

. . . As one parent demanded, "My kids know how to be
black—you all teach them how to be successful in the white
man's world."

—Lisa Delpit, *Other People's Children*

Once Sue, a red-haired Irish American from the Southside of Chicago, in-troduced me at a reading by saying that she thought she was white until she met me. "Now this girl is WHITE," she had said. She was right.

I was raised on Brooks Brothers and striped ties, Bass Weeguns and my fa-ther walking in the house in the evenings of my childhood with his leather briefcase and his London Fog thrown over his arm. But more than that, I was raised with *signals,* ways he frowned or turned his body slightly to the side in a subtle act of dismissal. I was raised to take in his looks and preferences. I was not always conscious of this. I was raised on Jane Austen. My mother put books by my bed and dressed me in round collars, plaid skirts, and sweaters with patterned yokes.

I knew, by the time I was in the summer of my fifteenth year, exactly how to speak to my boss, a neurologist who slept on the couch in his office some nights. I knew about *stance:* distance, silence, being discreet and off to the side. I learned these things because I was a white woman in a world where power was never spoken of but assumed. I grew up learning about the order of forks at the table, the carefully constructed signs and signals of the head-mistress of my boarding school, when to stand, when to sit. I *absorbed* this culture without realizing it.

Some of the students I teach, both black and white, were not raised with this. They recognize that I do have something useful to give them here. So they pay attention.

How we are raised

A LESSON IN THE WAYS OF THE POWER STRUCTURE

There are ten minutes left in the hour. I tell students that they can put away their work if they want and come to the back of the room for some more talk about jobs, interviews, vocational stuff. I have put up an article about this in my "topic of the week" selection board. Students can get credit for writing an essay about the article and also for talking about it. Some weeks no one wants to have the discussion, other weeks a few are interested. Today everyone except for Leah and a new student, Takisha, come back with me. Leah is working harder than I have ever seen her. She is writing about teens and pregnancy, about her mother taking care of her child, about how lucky she is. Because Leah feels lucky, I don't want to interfere with her at all. She has not mentioned Ramon or Leticia all hour.

Takisha says she already has a job and is not interested.

Josh asks me about going for an interview. The article talked about the importance of making a first impression and about how some applicants don't know how to do that.

"What do you wear?" he asks.

"I would just dress in what clothes you might wear to church or some slightly formal event."

"You, know, white people's clothes," says Tyrone. "Oh, no offense, Landsman."

"What do you mean? I don't dress like that." This from Josh, who is dressed in baggy pants and a T-shirt, similar to the clothes many of the others, both black

Don't know

94

and white, are wearing today. Meanwhile, Tyrone is dressed in a button-down shirt with pressed slacks. So much for racial definitions of dress.

"Just clothes that you would wear if you wanted to impress someone."

"You wear your church clothes, not your party clothes." Nancy says this.

"You got that right. Hey, speaking of parties, what time you gonna start on Saturday?" Tyrone asks.

"We're not speakin' of parties, really. This a job talk. Eight o' clock, though." Nancy says this and then nods toward me, giving me permission to continue.

I go on. "I would wear pressed pants, a clean dress shirt, a tie, and a jacket or sweater."

"Like this," says Tyrone, and in a rare moment of playfulness for him, he gets up and parades in front of the others.

"How about shoes?" Tamika asks.

"Tyrone, what did you wear when you interviewed at the post office the first time?"

"Church-type shoes," he says, "but then they don't care what you wear after that."

"You got any shoes you wear to church when you go?" I ask Jamal, who has wandered in and has joined the group.

"Yeah. Some ol' leather ones. You know, tie shoes. Ugly."

"Like my mom makes me wear." This from Josh. "Ugly ol' shoes."

They laugh. I have often found that almost all the students in my classes, be they in the suburbs or the city, have common tastes in clothes. Usually, black students wear the latest fashions first, then the white kids follow. Any suburban hallway will reveal the baggy pants, baseball cap, and starter jacket fashions of the cities as the predominant mode of dress among white students of all groups.

"What about clothes for us women?" asks Sarah.

"Not a sweater like that one you wearin' right now. They can see all the way down," says Nancy.

"So? Fine for them. They get a treat!"

"OOOOOOOOOOhhhhhhhhh," everyone in the group calls out.

"A dress or skirt or pants outfit. You know how to dress." I say this and she nods her head.

"Yeah. Like those white kids over Southwest High School be wearin'. Those little sweaters and white blouses and shit like that, huh, Landsman?" Tyrone asks this.

"Excuse the swearing," he adds quickly.

"You don't have to give up your own taste. Just think about where you are going, who is going to interview you. In an office you want to appeal to whites or blacks who might be the ones interviewing you; the ones who have the power to hire you or not. Or to anyone who wants their office to look kind of conservative."

"You mean boring, wants it to look boring," says Tamika. She rolls her eyes.

"What do you wear at the post office?" I ask Tyrone.

"Jus' what I got on. 'Cept when I go on delivery. Then I wear the uniform. Don't mind that, though. Then nobody out in Robbinsdale or Crystal stops me if I have the uniform on."

"Yeah. I put my uniform on *before* I go out to my wait job in Bloomington. Just so no one pulls me over before I get there and makes me late." Nancy says this.

"You waitin' tables? When you do that? I didn't know you doin' that?"

"Jus' started las' week. Got me a ol' car and I do the four to ten shift. Many times as I can get it."

"They let you wear the head covering?" I ask.

"Yeah. They don't seem to mind."

"What about braids, cornrows, and stuff?" Jamal asks. "What if they tell you you have to get rid of them?"

I have no answer for them here. There have been lawsuits in this state about just this issue, and the women who asked to be able to wear cornrows lost one case out at the Mall of America, where many of these students work. I ask them what they would do.

"I would look for another job," Tameka says. "I would not give up looking black for no job."

All of them nod their heads, including Josh and Sarah.

The door opens and Reggie walks in. He holds up a pink pass.

"It's okay, man. I got it changed and Jones said I could come down here." He walks back to the group. Alan, who has been helping Leah with her story, looks up.

"They really changed it?"

"Yeah, man, you don't believe me?" Reggie flashes angry. His stance becomes rigid.

"I believe you." Alan sits back down next to Leah.

"Okay then, the man believes me." Reggie talks himself down a little.

"What you all doin'?" he asks us.

That's crazy

"This is a job group. You know, interviewing and stuff." Tyrone says this.

"Why you need it, man, you already got a dumb job?"

"It ain't no dumb job, man. It pays enough for me to live over Northeast."

"Why you wanna live over in that ol' white place?" Reggie asks. He looks at me. "No offense." He looks back at Tyrone. "Why, man?"

"I would like to get back to the job interview," I say.

"There are lots of brothers over on the Northeast side, man."

"Those brothers tryin' to be white. Jus' like you."

"They are just trying to make it, Reggie," I say.

Tyrone does not say a word. He has tried arguing or explaining his hopes for the future and his desire to save money, to stay out of jail, before this discussion today. It has not worked. I can see that right now he does not want to get in a fight with Reggie. I silently applaud him for this and for all the days he has had to silence himself.

"I don't need no job talk," Reggie says, stomping back to the front of the room.

Alan gets up and goes to him. They talk softly. Reggie becomes calm.

A PLACE IN THE WHITE WORLD

They listen intently, eyes fixed on me.

I almost always get this kind of undivided attention when I am explaining how to interview for a job. I feel their concentration when I talk about answering questions, how to sit, what to say in a letter of introduction. I will not need to tell them this many times because this matters to them. If they do not pay attention, then they may not get the job, be accepted into the college. If they do not write the correct five-paragraph essay, they may not be awarded one of the few scholarships at the school where they want to go. In addition to the black students, white students like Josh and Sarah—those with too-small shoes and thin T-shirts, the ones who are often cold in the winter—listen with the same intensity as the students who are black, Native, Asian, and Latino/a.

In another school with a different kind of student population, I might not get this response. Even here at ASP there is a percentage of students whose parents have told them these same things about getting a job and keeping it. However, even in suburban schools and definitely here, there is a large group of students who simply do not know how to get help in order to go where they want to go, be accepted where they want to be accepted.

I also see more and more students who are recent immigrants to this country. If they are to be given entrée into the world of power in the United States, they will need to know the codes, the ways of dress, and the protocols of white power culture. I believe it is up to those of us in public education to be aware of this and to prepare these students, many of whom are not white, for a multitude of choices for their future.

The students here, in front of me now, are smart. Although they do live in a white world, many of them are not *of* that world. Yet they have carefully observed it. They have had to observe it in order to survive in it. They know they have to learn to negotiate between their own homes and mine. They have to learn to lower their voices and raise their hands. Some may have to speak without dialect. Like Preston, they may decide to immediately leave any room where they are left alone with valuable equipment. They use their observation and knowledge of the white world of power, combined with what we can tell them of this world, in order to negotiate their way.

 I feel that my role in this negotiation is tricky. I am only giving them part of the picture, the part I live, the part I observe from inside the culture. I can make explicit what I know about jobs and how to keep them, about finding homes, getting into college. I also feel a responsibility to make sure I do this *without asking them to give up anything of their own culture, their own language.*

Many students are bilingual. They speak white English and Ebonics. They speak Hmong or Spanish at home and English in school. They are always translating. Translation is more than just language translation. It is body language, eye contact, all the subtle things I grew up with in a rich white home. Many of the students I work with have already figured this out. Others are not so sure, and still others don't want to have anything to do with it all. For those who *do* want support in going out to find certain types of jobs, I believe that it is up to those of us who are a part of the white power world to give them all the information we can. This information, coupled with the observations they have already made, may enable them to flow a little more easily into white structures. This information, on how to take a test, on what are on the SATs, on how to study for essay exams, might simply be giving them more of a choice in competing for jobs in white corporations if this is what they are aiming for.

My other role is to subtly support those who are trying to make it outside their own peer group. The key word here is *subtly*. I cannot be seen as an ally yet can become one. If it is after school, or before, by passing a note or writing a job or college reference in secret, I feel I have to be there for those students who are aiming for something some of their peers will demean them for wanting. I have to be supportive of their "acting white," as their peers may call it, without singling them out. This is a tightrope that is difficult to walk. I slip too often. I give verbal praise aloud where too many can hear and the student is embarrassed. He knows he will have to put up with teasing later.

ROLE PLAYING

"So you get to the interview early, Landsman?" This from Tamika.

"I would just make sure you leave some time for something to go wrong. Like you miss your bus, or something."

"What if your baby is sick and you can't go to the interview?" Leah asks this from across the room. I did not realize she had been listening.

"Try to arrange for a back-up person to take care of him just in case." I know how hard this is, and yet it seems to make sense because they are all nodding their heads, including Tyrone.

I look over at Alan and Reggie. They are sitting with each other. Reggie calls to me, when he sees me looking.

"Can I write a letter to my cousin in prison, Landsman? Can it count for my autobiography thing about family?"

"Yes. I will have to read it, though, if that is alright. Just to check on grammar, spelling, and stuff."

"That's okay." He turns toward his screen. While I talk with the jobs group, he continues working, with Alan nearby if he has questions. At other times Alan ends up in a discussion with students at the end of the hour. Today, without speaking about it to each other, we have automatically decided he will stay with Leah and Reggie.

"So, how you 'sposed to talk, Landsman?"

"Just like you talk to me, in school. Polite. Respectful."

They nod their heads. They have had to speak two languages all their lives. Sarah and Josh, who are white, as well as Reggie, Tyrone, and Leah, have learned to use both street language and school language since they were young. Their parents have often demanded polite language in their homes, and they have learned the language of the streets themselves. Sometimes there is no difference between the language on the streets and that used in their homes. I believe we simply need to acknowledge these two languages. They understand perfectly how to speak "school" and know that this would be required on certain jobs.

"I'm the boss, you are sitting before me, wanting a job," I say. "Who wants to try it?" Sarah raises her hand.

"How do you do, Ms. Mitchell. My name is Mr. Thomas. Would you like to sit down?"

"I already sitting down, dork man!" says Sarah, and of course we all laugh.

"Naw, Landsman, I'm for real now."

"Okay. Let's try this again. How do you do. Ms. Mitchell, isn't it? Would you like to sit down?"

"How do you do. Thank you. I would be privileged and honored to take a seat in your lovely office." Sarah puts on a fake British accent when she says these words. Her back is ramrod straight and her mouth pinched. There is a gleam in her eyes. The group laughs again.

"For real, huh?" I ask her after we settle down again.

"Okay. Okay."

I repeat the introductions. This time she speaks in a more normal tone.

"Yes. Thank you."

"Now." I look at some imaginary paper work in front of me. "You are almost finished with your high school work. Have you worked on a computer, Ms. Mitchell?"

"Yes. But they are kind of old and raggedy at my school."

"I would not admit that, necessarily," I say, stepping out of character. "I would just tell him you have worked on computers and can be trained easily."

"Awwright. Let me try again, Landsman."

We go on through the interview. The others do not fidget, as we talk about her experience in a few previous jobs or about her problems finding a place to live and her plans for college. No one interrupts. Then the interview is over and we shake hands. I tell her I will be calling her soon to let her know. We all sit back, relieved.

"That seems so hard, Landsman."

"What makes it hard?" I ask.

Filter

"You know, always having to watch how you talk," Sarah answers. They nod their heads.

"I don't know what to say," I tell them. "I think it really will get easier. And you won't have to be this careful all the time. Just when you are getting the job and working in certain places. Also, talk to your parents about this. Many of them have to change how they talk when they go into their jobs. Ask them how they negotiate it. And you do it all the time, at school." I have been lazy. In other years in similar situations I would have invited parents in to talk about their jobs.

"It ain't so bad after you get used to it," Tyrone says. "In the mail room I can talk any way, really. Don't matter about how I talk until I go out to deliver."

Someone mentioned to me the other day that we all speak in dialects: academic lingo, artistic language, and medical terminology. It just so happens that the language that those of us in the white upper or middle classes often grow up with is the language of power. Dialects and vocabularies are not neutral or equal in weight. Some are more powerful in the day-to-day working world than others. Those in power often view their own way of speaking as superior and, at the same time, as the standard.

The students I have worked with over the years simply want a chance to learn the language of power. From what I can tell, they have no intention of giving up their dialects, their accents, or their culture. In giving them what information I have at my disposal, I do not believe I am asking them to deny anything; rather, I am adding a new vocabulary for some, and for others I am simply reinforcing what they have learned from their parents, mentors, or pastors. And yet, I will continue to feel uncomfortable about this, as though I am criticizing the way they speak in their homes.

It is almost time for the hour to end. I tell them they can talk for a few minutes before the bell rings.

I walk over to talk to Reggie. "How you doing?"

"Awwright. You want to read what I got so far?"

"Yes." We print it out and I walk back to my desk, sit down, and read:

Cuz,

How you doin, man? I am planning on coming to see you next weekend if my lady don't give me no grief over it. I am still with Lilana and her baby. My baby. We doin all right. I need to get a job that pays me some more money, though. Makes me tempted to do the dealing thing again, but I don't want to. I miss you, man. I keep remembering that night they got you, how they took you.

Some times I remember when we were younger and I want it to be like that again, you know cuz? How we didn't have to have no jobs, and rode our bikes all over the projects and our mothers hollered at us at night. Comin in late, Getting into little shit. Nothing big, though.

Moms is okay. Jus don't see her since I got my own crib over on the Northside. My homes are doin alright and you know, everything else is cool right now.

The bell rings. Reggie walks toward the door.

"This is good!" I call to him. "Just keep going. Try to think of some more memories." I do like what he has written. It is a good entrée, too, into talking about audience, who we write for, how our audience changes the language we use. Next, maybe I will ask him to write a more formal letter, to a boss, a college.

Reggie smiles just for a split second. Then he begins to saunter, shrugs his shoulders. His body changes as he leaves. I feel that just under the surface of Reggie's bravado is Reggie's desire to do well. Sometimes I can make it through to that person. Other times I seem to fail, no matter how hard I try. Right now I cannot tell which way it will go with him.

The rest of the students get up from their seats at the back of the room. They walk out, slowly, barely saying good-bye. I go to stand by the door, to watch classes pass. I am supposed to be out there between each class. Yet I find there are usually a few students who want to talk, finish up an essay. Or a new student comes in. It has always been a problem, this being in two places at once that is teaching.

I guess it is kind of like the students' lives sometimes, being two people: the work person with the work language; while at the same time, being the person who speaks differently at home, to friends, at parties, at reunions. While I do not like this double life, this "whitening" of culture, I know something about the students' reality from what they have written or told me. So I continue, once in awhile, to talk about play acting, assuming a role. Some already do this, and for some there is no conflict. They come to me with this knowledge. They do not talk "street" at all. For those who feel they need it, though, I walk a strange line of teaching them to negotiate and urging them not to give up their language, their culture.

REFLECTION QUESTIONS

1. What are inclusive ways we can make sure students from varying cultures are provided with entrée into the world of power in the United States?

What can we do without denigrating their language or culture? Students often want this knowledge yet teachers are reluctant to address these skills. Why do you think this is?

2. If we speak of "translating" student language into language the college, employer, or professor wants, this pays respect to both languages our students speak. This includes black English. Why are some teachers reluctant to put it in these terms? How can we provide experiences for students to use their home or street language in creative ways in the classroom?

3. All dialects and languages are certainly not equal in this country. How can we communicate that we know this to students while making sure they know we respect the way they speak, the way their mother and grandmother, father and grandfather speak?

4. What are some ways to address the inequity that can empower students?

11

SIXTH HOUR

Expectations

Just the thought of being numbered and labeled makes each of us, I think, want to rebel; the poisonous impact of casual categorization (at least when applied to ourselves) causes us to recoil. And yet schools are built on labeling, categorizing, sifting and sorting.

— Bill Ayers, *Off White*

Interesting

OF ADULTS

Alan stands next to me at our classroom door. A young man is coming down the hall toward us. He has on a bandanna. We do not allow our students to wear head coverings. Such coverings often indicate gang colors, and colors can provoke violence. We do not even allow them to wear hats with brims, as the direction of the brim can illustrate gang affiliation.

"Oh, man," Alan says, shaking his head. "I've got to ask that young man to take off his bandanna."

"I think it's my turn," I say. "I think you asked someone on Tuesday."

"No. You've been doin' it all week. And I know what he's gonna do, too. He's gonna say something like: 'Who you talkin' to, man? I ain't gonna take my rag off for no one.'"

"And then you'll have to take him down to the office and there will be a scene and you will get to your next job late," I say, shaking my head, anticipating the often repeated scenario. "I'll do it, honest."

Alan holds up his hand to me. As the young man approaches us, Alan stops him quietly.

"You just can't wear that in the building, man. You know the rules."

The student looks sullen, distant. I wince, thinking it is going to get loud, explosive. All of a sudden, he reaches up to touch his head. He looks startled and immediately takes off the bandanna.

"Sorry, man," he says to Alan. "I forgot."

"That's okay but don't forget again, okay, man?" Alan smiles. The student smiles. He walks away, shaking his head at his own memory lapse.

Alan looks at me. I laugh. We shrug our shoulders.

We do this all the time. We see a kid who has a certain look: baggy pants, long shirts, high tops, bandanna, and we decide exactly how he or she will behave. And not just the white staff. Black teachers and support staff learn to assume behaviors, too. We lower our expectations without realizing it. In this case it was quite harmless. At other times, in other contexts, though, our low expectations can deprive students of an education, a future, hope.

Natural lower expect.

If I had to state the most important thing I have learned from my colleagues who are not white, it would be in this area of expectations. They constantly remind me to expect the students I work with to follow rules about the hallways and the classroom. They remind me I must also demand that students get their homework in, speak up in class, and read long novels, science texts, and historical accounts.

A group of black students from a nearby high school visited a university class in Urban Education I was teaching and talked with us about the way teachers treat them. I have included their words here because they echo in my head as I think about this crucial area of our teaching.

"White teachers show they are afraid of us. They try to be too nice. And you know, Landsman, we take what we get. You all got to tell us what you all want from us."

"Yeah, you watch some of those mean ol' teachers. Specially the black ones. They tell us what to do, no foolin' around. Even some white teachers do this. Shows they respect us, Landsman. Shows they expect we know how to behave."

Expectations

"Yeah. Other teachers. They are sweet and all. But it doesn't seem like they really treat us like we can behave. Like we can do the work. Seem they let us go on and mess up."

I think of parents: for them, too, the easy way is often the permissive way. My husband and I were stricter than many of our friends when we were raising our son. We expected him home for dinner, expected him to call when he was going to be late. We pushed him to get his homework done. I believe that students who talk to me about teachers, and expectations, simply want what our son wanted: that we tell him straight out what we expect and tell him when he is "messing up." And while I think this is hard, especially to softies like myself, love demands this, for students as well as for our own children.

I watch the crowds in the hall going by me now, heading for the last class of the day. Sarah gives me a hug as she goes out of my room, on her way to the drinking fountain.

"I'm comin' back in to do some more work, okay?" She smells like cologne and peppermint as she bends close to me. I nod to her, and she smiles. Her body feels thin next to my body, which is solid and spreading with middle age.

OF PEERS

Preston is coming down the hall. A young black man tries to stop him. Preston pushes beyond him, comes a little closer to the door of my room. Before he gets much further, he is stopped again, this time by another young man, Dion, also black. Dion walks up next to Preston, his face near Preston's face. Preston, while staring straight ahead, says something and Dion turns away, muttering. By the time Preston gets to where I am standing, he has been stopped five times. Each time he has shrugged someone off, said something clever, or simply pushed on by. Finally, he arrives at my door, walks to his corner by the computer where he usually works, and collapses in the chair.

"Just let me chill a minute, Landsman," Preston says when I walk toward him. I nod and go back out in the hallway.

Peer pressure is different for Preston than for many other high school students. Because the complicated factors of race, poverty, and joblessness impact black students more severely than whites due to the racial divide in our segregated city, this kind of pressure is harder for Preston than for a middle-class white kid. He has no money except what he earns. Dealing drugs and being in a gang were attractive to him at one time, especially when he was hungry. When his former gang members are trying to enlist him again, it is dangerous for him to resist, more so than for a young white middle-class man who is being hassled for being a "nerd." And in all threats and taunts made against Preston, guns are implicit.

Students often talk about this. They talk about pressure "from the brothers" to skip school. They have to negotiate with their peers every day. If they decide to stay in school, they are accused of "acting white." If they skip, they know they are giving up their real belief and hope in a future. They also know they are hurting their parents, many of whom have sacrificed for them.

"White teachers don't get it sometimes," says Kevin, who is entering eleventh grade at a local high school in the fall. "They think you just have to tell your friends you can't skip with them, you got to go to class. And that's supposed to do it. But that ain't it. Later you deal with it on the street."

Kevin says it was actually worse in middle school. He remembers skipping school in eighth grade even though he knew he was not supposed to leave. He did this once in awhile just so he wouldn't be taunted by other black students for trying to be a good student.

"Parents get it, sometimes. They know they got to make a scene. They know they got to make it so the brothers see that you're in trouble at home if you hang out too much. So they do this scene and the brothers see how crazy your parents are and they don't hassle you so much if you don't go out with them to the mall all the time. Some white teachers do that, too. They make a scene if you skip class or something. Even though you pretend to be angry and all, you know they be helpin' you out."

"Yeah, but I think white teachers scared to make a scene." This from Leticia, also entering eleventh grade. "They scared to come up in your face sometimes."

I look back in the room. Preston is still sitting in his chair, head thrown back. In a similar situation to Tyrone, he is having a rough time at this alternative school. He is a gifted student who has been passed by, or who has passed school by when he was younger. He is getting As now. Many gang members who manage to stay in regular high schools get As. Teachers in mainstream high schools often tell me that some of the best students are leaders of gangs. Because we cannot put the two concepts together—gang member and A-student—we do not see these young men as the gifted individuals that they are. If they can make it through middle school and ninth grade, they may be able to graduate. Here at

ASP there are too many young men who have given up on the regular system and come to our school primarily to organize, recruit, and deal drugs.

Yet there are still many more Prestons here than we recognize. Many of the toughest-looking young men I have taught have turned out to be the best students. They need our support, our high expectations. They need us to make a scene about them and "come up in their face," as Leticia says.

OF INSTITUTIONS

Across from my room is the special education room. Outside it now, young black men and women stand, waiting for the teacher to open her door. There is not one white face in the group. This is also true in large high schools all over the country. For years black students were put into special education classes almost automatically, the assumption being that they would all need help because they would not be smart enough or would not have parents smart enough to get them to read at an early age. There are African-American professors who teach at Harvard now who, in elementary school, were put into classes for retarded students, based solely on the color of their skin. Although this has changed somewhat, in many districts these assumptions are still made. A few years ago one school in Rockford, Illinois, assumed that all Latino/a students would need to be screened for special education the minute they walked in the door.

The students who sit in my teacher education class can *feel* the low expectations even though it is difficult for them to articulate what is going on.

"My friend, she's real smart. She decided she wanted to go to the magnet for Liberal Arts where all the white kids were. Man, she had a hard time from the teachers, students, her friends." This from Kevin again. He shakes his head. "I ain't up for that, man, no matter how smart I am."

"It's the teachers," says Leticia. "They look at you a certain way, not like the way they look at white kids. They talk to you different, too. Like you can't hear so good."

Kevin and Leticia laugh. "Like you deaf or somethin', just because you're black."

"No, man. They just get more angry when you raise your hand than when some white girl raises hers. Or they talk down to you. Either that or they don't explain nothin' to you at all. Some of 'em can't even teach, man. They not used to you so they get angry or somethin'. I don't know."

Often schools are places where, because teachers lack cultural understanding, some children are reprimanded or criticized when they try to express

Know your students

themselves. Others are told to look the teacher in the eye when, in their culture, this is a sign of disrespect. And many times children are put into competitive situations, when they have been raised to work much harder and more effectively in cooperative groups.

When this happens on a school-wide or a university-wide level, it is institutional racism of a most insidious kind. We who are raised to speak quietly, to face our teachers directly, or to work on our own assume that the way we learned is the best way for all kids to learn. Because we are comfortable with learning in silence and solitude, we assume our students are comfortable like this. Because we have been encouraged to think of ourselves first and our community, or even our family, second, we assume the same values on the part of the kids we teach.

What is so unfortunate, in addition to what this does to students of color, is what it does to us white people. We are closed off from different and creative ways of looking at the world or from unique ways of working together. I realized this when I noticed that the thing I missed the most, when I went off to work in a primarily white suburban high school for the arts, was the humor, the give and take, the honesty of inner-city students, both white and black.

During teacher training we are taught primarily to work with white, middle-class students. So when we come to teach classes and find a majority of black, *Not trained* Native-American, Hmong, or Latino/a students in front of us, we are unnerved at first, sometimes uncomfortable. We refer these students out of our classrooms, to Special Education, simply because of this discomfort.

I sincerely believe it is time we get comfortable. It is time we train educators to get the jokes, welcome the dialogue, encourage the debate, and deal with all kinds of kids, both in the hallways and in the classroom.

When I turn to look back in the room, Preston has fallen asleep. His head is against the chair, his book open, his floppy disk in the computer. As I glance around at my sixth hour, I see, right before me, the way educational institutions have failed black, Asian, Native, and Latino/a students. I see this, because ASP is a school of last resort. Students come here who have not made it in the regular schools. And here, in this building, where they come for specialized, individualized help, there are 90 percent students of color. Yet 75 percent of them can read perfectly, can write clearly, and can reason in a sophisticated, adult way.

So why are they here? I can only conclude that somewhere along the line, our community and our system have not found ways to reach them. We cannot discount the importance of parents, home life, money, and street influences, and I do not expect any school system to act as surrogate parents, ministers, and guardians for all the students who come through its doors. Yet I also believe that we can reach these students much sooner, and keep them coming to regular schools, by making them welcome.

Kevin and Leticia have told me that some white teachers are good at welcoming.

"Sometimes white teachers are good. They are the ones who tell you to be in their rooms after school. They help you study and they keep an eye on you." Kevin smiles and looks at Jill Costa, his white Social Studies teacher who accompanied the group.

"Even after you're done with them and moving on, they keep an eye on you."

"Yeah, they are on you, man, like they think they're your gramma, or some-thin'." Kevin looks at Jill again. They laugh.

"They teach more like black people teach." This from John. He is in the Liberal Arts Magnet, which includes a large percentage of white students.

"Yeah. They tell you they want the work done, they want you to be polite, they want you to stay after. They call you on your shit. They know your con," Kevin says.

Not all

As I continue to stand by the door, watching for late students, Sarah comes back by me. She waves a book in my face. It is by Ursula LaGuinn.

"Can I read this all hour? I'll write a book review when I am done."

"Sure," I tell her. She walks to the back of the room, stopping to pinch Preston on the cheek to wake him up, and curls up on the blue couch to read. She will not move until it is time for her to go home.

I must admit that my first impulse is often to wonder why a girl who looks like Sarah has arrived in my classroom at ASP. Yet when I see a young black man come in in baggy clothes, a long shirt, and a bandanna hanging out of his pocket, I do not question his arrival in this special site. And similarly, when I worked in a series of regular city high schools, I was not surprised when I went by the vocational education wing, the shop class, and the auto body garage to see black, Native-American, and poor white students working on small engines or on transmissions. There were rarely any female students in those rooms. I accepted this for years.

At some point my easy acceptance of such assumptions began to bother me. Even now, after all these years, my reaction to new students at ASP bothers me. It seems almost as if I must stop something as automatic as breathing, as taking air in and out of my lungs, to stop my mind from expecting behavior from kids according to skin color, clothing, cleanliness, or speech.

I hear loud swearing from the end of the hallway. Coming around the corner, a new white student is yelling obscenities at the counselor. She stomps down the corridor in new thick-soled boots, her dress immaculate, stylish. From her outward appearance she could be a cheerleader out in the suburbs. I try to stop my initial impulse of surprise at her presence.

OF "GIFTED" PROGRAMS

I get ready to close my door. I see two young men, one white and one black, standing in the hall reciting song lyrics. They are performing as a duet, back and forth. They are good. A few students poke their heads out of their classrooms to listen.

Where is the program, where has been the program, that recognizes their gifts? Where is the program that also recognizes that one of them might love to learn more about Mozart? Where is the program that welcomes them as the gifted young men they are, insists they learn Shakespeare sonnets, points out similarities in British rhythm poems and popular music? In many cities, including Minneapolis, programs for "gifted" high school students are often filled only with whites. In grade schools this is not the case. Many teachers in both elementary and middle schools are creating gifted programs for students of all cultures. Yet the definitions of giftedness, even in the earlier grades, are often definitions that reward the strengths of white, middle-class students.

All of our students have gifts—Preston, Sarah, Sheila, and Leah. Until our system of education, as a whole system, recognizes this, then the programs we create, with the labels that become fixed on students from the earliest grades, seem almost dangerous. We continually define giftedness using measures of a certain kind of verbal ability, or we base entrance into programs for gifted students on traditional academic grade-point averages. Recently in St. Paul, a group of white parents became upset when the measurement for entrance into gifted programs was changed to a new test that would make students of limited English proficiency eligible for consideration. These parents worry me a great deal.

At a recent "diversity" program one of the trainers, who is white, did not agree with my concern that gifted programs tend to be another way of exclusion of students of color. She told me that we needed gifted programs to keep white kids in city schools. I was shocked. She was surrounded by a wonderfully diverse and gifted group of adults, but her statement implied that *gifted* meant *white.*

In some Minneapolis high schools, the only program for gifted students is the International Baccalaureate Program. This program is Eurocentric in content. Students who are not white are often made to feel unwelcome in IB. As a result, in many schools *the only gifted program is a white program.*

When Kevin and John talk about this, they talk about personality differences, not differences in ability.

"John is a 'jeller,'" says Kevin.

John smiles.

"A 'jeller'?"

"Someone who can get along with anybody. He jels, man."

"Do you have to be like that to get along in the Liberal Arts Magnet for gifted students, then?"

"Oh, yeah. If you black, you do. You got to ignore a lot of white shit, and black shit from the brothers who want to know why you in there."

"If there were more black students in these programs, would it be easier then?"

"Yeah."

"Then you wouldn't have to be all alone. Man, I hate it when I am the only one in the room."

"Would it help if there were black teachers as part of these programs?"

"Yeah. I guess. I would always want more black teachers. But if you got to have all white teachers, and you have a teacher like Miss Costa, you can make it."

Jill Costa smiles.

This racial perception of who is gifted is exemplified by the situation of John Hope Franklin. He is a gifted black historian, Pulitzer Prize–winner, and head of the President's Commission on Race. Two years ago, walking into a hotel to be part of a ceremony at which he was to receive an award for his scholarship and writing in African American History, a woman stopped him in the lobby. She handed him her coat, assuming he was the coat-check man.

By ways as subtle as how we define gifted and as glaring as automatically referring all Latino/a students to special education, we perpetuate the racist restrictions that limit our students, whether they are Latino/a, black, Asian, Native American, or white. I am convinced that when gifted classes are mixed in proportion to the cultural mix of the school and the district, we will have real equity in gifted education.

I begin sixth hour, and everyone is finally settled at a computer. I am convinced that Preston is an original thinker; he could run for office and win. Sarah could write mysteries or perhaps become a teacher. And there is Monty Jackson, a new student, who is reading *Star Trek* stories and writing some of his own. He could be a scientist.

Tyrone could be a novelist, a teacher, a president. He has recently tested off the charts in math. His scores are so high, they place him over the top of most students nationally. I am not unrealistic about his potential, about the possibilities for him. Rather, it is an entire system that has labeled him as "lacking potential" that is unrealistic.

So now I claim realism. I claim it when I say that Sheila could go to college and beyond and end up getting a law degree. I claim realism when I believe my nephew, who has a learning disability in reading but who is brilliant in math, could become a professor of mathematics someday. Because he is white and middle class, he certainly has a better shot at a career that matches his potential.

The students who sit in front of me now will have the obstacles of entrenched labels, categorization, and institutional racism challenging them all the way, defining what is "realistic" for them. When Malcom X's teacher told him he should consider being a custodian instead of a scientist, she deprived him of hope. This kind of oppression still goes on, in the name of realism, of being "honest with students about their limitations." It is as insidious as any law, as damaging as any written policy. Without constant advocacy on the part of parents and teachers, many students who are gifted or who could be college-bound will be left to despair, to feel hopeless, to find themselves in schools defined as places for "losers."

OF CLASSROOM TEACHERS

I close the door. I like the sound it makes behind me, the quiet that settles over the entire room. It is 1:30. Outside there is a hum of cars, but mostly sound is muted. I pull down the large shades that cover one whole wall of windows, and the light becomes soft.

Alan begins to walk around, as I do, asking if anyone has any questions. A new student, Dante, comes in. He is tall and muscular and wears gold chains around his neck. His skin is copper brown. He has on a wool cap. I get him started at the computer, ask him about his previous school.

Tyrone is busy at his spot, writing an autobiography. Sara is lost in her book. Jamar is trying to think of something to say about hunger and homelessness.

They are concentrating. Leah comes in to work some more and sits next to Dante. Alan is helping Preston think of what to say on an essay question for a scholarship.

Suddenly, out of the blue, "What you lookin' at, ho?" This from Dante.

"I ain't lookin', man. Jus' seein' if you got the computer right," Leah answers back, calmer than I have heard her. Yet the tension under this calmness is almost palpable.

"Keep your eyes on your work, bitch."

I walk toward them as Leah gets ready to fire back. Before she can, and before I can say anything, Tyrone says, quietly, "Hey, man, you can't use *bitch* and *ho* in here. She don't let you talk that way, man." He gestures toward me.

Preston speaks up next, "Yeah, man. She says she can't tell you what you can say in the hallway 'less she hears you out there, but you can't say *bitch* and *ho* in here."

Dante looks at me. I nod my head. Alan nods his head at Dante.

"Shit, man." Dante turns back toward his computer.

Leah mumbles under her breath, and I am sure it will all start again. But it doesn't. Alan raises his eyebrows as we signal each other.

I know he is saying to me: "Not bad."

We both know we have to work on words like *shit* with Dante, but now he has gotten one point very well. We did not have to say a thing. Finally, it seems that our expectations for how we treat each other in this room have become the same for the students here.

After half the hour is over, I ask if students want to talk about a topic. I decide that we will talk about the question of expectations. Everyone decides to join in on the discussion except for Preston, who is deep into writing his story.

"Don't no one expect nothin' from me but myself. Not my parents, not my girlfriend." Dante says this.

"How about school? Any of you feel high expectations in your school years?"

They are silent. I wait.

Finally, Tyrone says, "Sometimes. Like in first grade there was this one white teacher who liked all us kids, even the ones in the projects. She laughed all the time with us, you know. It felt okay in that room, like she was down for you, you know?"

"Like Miss Carter in the third grade. Man, she was a mean black lady but she don't let no one mess with any of 'her kids.' She tough. All them spellin' words."

some are needed

"I had her, man. She used to call my ma all the time about me."

"How about expectations now?" Alan asks this.

"I feel like someone expect somethin' from me when I go to my gramma's house. She makes me come on Saturdays and she don't let me go outside 'til I have done all my homework. She's real strict," says Josh, who is also back this hour.

"You think that is good, her being strict?" I ask.

"Yeah, man. Real good. You got to be strict with us, you know. We try to get over on you with all sorts of shit and stuff, and you got to catch us, man. Oh, excuse the language, Landsman."

Leah says, "He's right, man. We need that kind of no bullshit stuff. My gramma used to be that way, man. Now she dead."

I often find myself in trouble with those I know who want to build classrooms around giving power over to the students. These educators work well with motivated students, black and white, Asian and Latino/a, from middle-class homes. I am not sure how well this philosophy goes with students whose lives are full of chaos, whose homes are somewhat tense, and who themselves are filled with indecision. I also know that many wealthy suburban students I worked with at the High School for the Arts for a few years wanted structure. They never really said this to me, but I could sense it. They almost seemed relieved when I provided guidelines and rules.

strict

"White teachers be afraid to tell us to be quiet. They say like 'Would you please be quiet now so we can get some work done in here?' They just need to tell us, not ask us, 'Be quiet or you all stay after.' Or somethin' like that." Kevin says this as the students and Jill struggle to define what it is that white teachers need to learn.

"Like sometimes you want the teacher to say, 'You need to do this and then this and then this.' Instead they want to give you all these choices and stuff."

"I like choices sometimes. Just not about how I behave and all. I want the teacher to tell students around me they talkin' too much and stuff. Not ask them to be quiet. Tell them to be quiet. Then let me choose my book I want to read or something like that." This from Leticia.

"You got to feel the teacher is in control." John says this. "You got to feel that to feel safe in there."

In class, Tyrone changes the topic to safety.

"My protectors are my friends sometimes. When they take my back I feel safe. But that ain't all the time, Landsman."

"So school is only sometimes safe?"

"Never safe now, man." This from Sam. "Everything go on in school that goes on in the streets."

They all nod their heads in unison.

I tell them about Maslow's hierarchy of needs. It says that you need certain things before you can learn and that often, if you don't have these things, you will not be able to study, you will not be curious, you will not want to use your full potential. I say that first you need food, drink, sleep, sex, and other survival necessities. Then you need safety. To be free from danger and anxiety, you need security. Once you have these needs met, you can go on to love and then self-respect. And so on.

They are fascinated, especially by the idea that sex is a basic need along with food and drink.

"I know that's right!" says Tyrone.

"I think I got it backward, then. I need respect before I need to eat, man. Somebody dis me and I don't care about nothin' but gettin' my respect back. You know what I mean?"

This is Dante, my new student. I am already beginning to like him. I like people who refuse to believe the experts.

"Yeah. Well, it is hard to concentrate on much when you always lookin' over your shoulder." Tyrone says this as he gets up to put away his notebook. The others agree with him and get ready to leave.

"What would make this school safe, any school safe?" I ask.

They stop for a moment before heading to stand at the door to the hall.

"Get you some metal detectors," says Josh.

"Keep the gangsters the hell outta here." This comes from Preston, who has turned off his computer and has come up to the front of the room.

"Man, what you sayin'? Gangsters got a right to an education, man." This comes from Jamar, who has been quiet, listening the entire time.

I jump in, the way I usually do because I cannot stand tension and do not want this to continue out in the hallway.

"Maybe it is just that everyone has a right to a *safe* education, that they are expected to leave their gang affiliation at the door along with their weapons when they come in."

"Yeah," Preston says, "like no colors and no hats. That kinda stuff."

"Okay. Man, I see what you're sayin', man, okay now."

The bell rings.

OF COUNSELORS, ADMINISTRATION

My regular day is almost over. I have a meeting with Tyrone and his counselor; then on to a class I am teaching at a nearby university. Tonight I will have to return to school before going home, because there are final conferences for parents.

I head down the hall to the conference room. Tyrone is there, impatient to go to his job. The counselor, John, an older white man, is there. So are the rest of Tyrone's teachers, all white men.

John tells us about Tyrone's high test scores. He mentions his exceptional math and language abilities on standardized tests. I chime in with comments about how much Ty has been reading and writing. I tell them all I think he is a writer. Two of the other teachers barely nod their heads. They seem lifeless and yet restless, checking their watches. Another man, Marvin, says he believes Tyrone has done exceptional work. He is proud of Ty's efforts and how quickly he has finished his math objectives.

I smile at Marvin. We have rarely talked, but I feel we share something. The rest are men I have seen at other conferences for Tyrone. These are the men who have refused to give him any leeway in doing his work. They have consistently told me, in asides in the hallways, that these kids are all headed for jail, anyway, "so what's the purpose of working so hard, Julie?" These are the same men who sit in the back of faculty meetings and read the newspaper or grumble under their breaths at any new requirement. They are men who are biding their time until retirement, who have been in the profession too long.

They are still a part of the educational system. And they should not be. In this case they are white and male. I have met teachers like them from every culture, with every color of skin, of both genders. Until we as a profession cease defending them, we are not going to gain credibility in the larger community.

I know this stand may make me unpopular with my colleagues. And with principals. Because I believe it is the administrators in our schools who have let us down the most. These men and women are charged with running a school, evaluating a staff, and monitoring teachers. Yet time and again, they seem to turn the other way when incompetence is apparent or even when students are being mistreated. They blame the unions, and the unions blame the administrators.

In the best schools, principals and teachers work in alliance for kids. The good teachers are supported, the ones who are not making it are given help and then asked to consider another career if they cannot become effective. We need creative leadership from administrators at all levels who are also trained to promote inclusiveness, to understand white privilege, and to encourage cultural awareness.

Kids can tell you all about teachers who should not be in the classroom. Kevin talked about one teacher who refused to help him with his math.

"He just walked on by my desk when my hand was up. I think he does this to make me mad. Then I get angry and he gets to kick me out."

"Yeah. He does that." Leticia nods her head. "Some of them they don't want to answer your question. They look so annoyed at you and shake their heads as though you're dumb. But they never explain it, neither."

"Bottom line: they don't like you. They don't like no body, especially black students. That's the bottom line." They all nod their heads.

A previous principal of ASP told me once that within two weeks of arriving at this school, students can tell which teachers like them and which teachers do not. They know exactly who will help them and exactly who will make them suffer, without assistance, through the credits necessary to graduate.

The conference for Tyrone is almost over.

"What do you suggest, then, for Tyrone after he graduates in a few weeks?" I ask.

John looks up. "Well, I have been talking to him about vocational school. Maybe St. Paul Technical College or Brown Institute."

"Why not college? Metro State, the University?"

Except for Marvin, the men shake their heads.

"I don't think so. Tyrone, do you have the money for college? Is that what you want?"

Tyrone, who is often eloquent, shrugs his shoulders and is silent.

"I am not sure why he should rule it out," I say.

"I agree." This from Marvin. "Tyrone's scores are high enough. He would have no trouble in a college program."

"Tyrone?" John looks at him. He is gathering up his papers, his tests, his scores, and his folders. I cannot believe he is just going to leave it there. I am furious.

"I don't know yet." Tyrone stands up. "I need to think about it, check it out."

"Talk to Alan," I suggest as we move toward the door. "He goes to Metro State. He can tell you what you need to do for a scholarship or something. He'll be here tonight for parent conferences."

Tyrone nods and heads down the stairs.

CHAPTER 11

As I turn around to walk back toward my room, a teacher grabs me by the arm.

"I think you are being unfair to suggest college to Tyrone."

"What do you mean?" I ask. "His test scores and skills are—"

"He doesn't have the motivation or the money," he interrupts me.

"I think he does have the motivation, actually. He just needs to *believe* he has it."

This man turns away. The counselor, John, who has heard this conversation, nods his head. I am not sure if he is agreeing with me or with the other teacher.

John has done some good things for students. He has gotten them into two-year and vocational schools. On rare occasions he has encouraged some to go on to four-year colleges. I am not sure why he has not suggested this for Tyrone today.

As I pass his desk, he looks up, annoyed. I nod my head and keep on going.

Marvin stops me in the hall. He shakes his head, talks about how discouraged he feels some days. He believes Tyrone would do fine at Metro.

I believe the Prestons and the Tyrones, the Dantes and the Jamars, the Leahs and the Sarahs, need to be challenged to think way beyond what they might even imagine for themselves. Just as they need to be expected to study Shakespeare, Freud, and European culture so they will not be lost in many colleges, they also need to be expected to dream of these colleges at all.

Challenge

Marvin and I do agree. We are two of many teachers who agree on this. We are two of legions of good teachers who push kids, prod them, plead with them, talk with them, work with them every day of the year both before and after school. There are many of us out here. I am not exceptional in my confidence in students. I think teachers desperately need to make alliances with each other, encourage each other to go on.

Eventually, students will tell you how much you meant to them. They will come back to visit, stay after school, or arrive at your door early in the morning, opening it for you as you struggle with your briefcase full of ungraded papers and your cup of coffee from McDonald's. They will say, without putting it into words, that you were exactly what they needed: an advocate.

"We need teachers who be down for us, no matter what." Kevin says this as John agrees.

"They don't gotta be nice all the time either. But we gotta know we can start over with them. Like our parents, I guess. Only they not our parents."

John, Leticia, and Kevin have put their finger on the tricky place teachers fill in their students' lives these days. We are their advocates, yet also their disciplinarians. We laugh with them, and yet we have to set limits with them. We must make them feel welcome, offer them books and pictures, music and ideas that will stimulate them, yet also make them feel our disappointment when they don't show up, come late, or slough off on a test. We walk a strange line, and often we are not part of their community, are not of their same culture.

To do all this, teachers need support: whether in the form of small class sizes, textbooks, technology, science supplies, paper, and pens, or money for field trips and visiting artists. We need this in all our schools, not only in places where white, affluent students go, but even more urgently in inner-city schools where students of color and poor students are in the majority. There are ways to redefine "realistic expectations" for all students, and one of those ways is to support the teachers who believe in them, who dream with them, who try to convince them they should stop at nothing.

We also need the support and advice of the parents of our students. If we are not expecting enough, we need to be told that. If we are missing something important in a student's life that may be interfering with his or her work, we need to be told that, too. If we have said anything that is offensive or asked something of a student that is not appropriate, given his cultural or religious values, we need to be informed.

We also need to be backed up when we ask students to get in homework, write papers, and study for tests. If we work in tandem with each other—parents, students, teachers, and others in the community—we can provide an education that does expect great things from each student in our classes and that does respect, and welcome, the potential in all of them.

REFLECTION QUESTIONS

1. What do teachers expect of their students? What leads to these expectations? Think of some subtle ways we may communicate expectations, either positive or negative. Given that we live in a society that presents us with negative images of people of color at every turn, what can we do about this as teachers?

2. What do you think students meant in this chapter when they said that being tough is a way of showing you are not racist? How is this tied into expectations?

3. How can we "make a scene" to take some of the pressure off students who are trying to do well?

4. What are some preconceived notions you have about who are in the programs for students in trouble? Are you surprised when upper-middle-class students show up in alternative programs in great numbers? Why?

5. Look at your school or one in your community or the one you attended. Is it tracked? Who is in the gifted track? Who is in the lower track? What color skin do these students have? Has your school re-segregated as so many have?

6. Think of ways schools perpetuate racial hierarchies, putting whites "on top" while students of color are relegated to less demanding classes. How can we break this pattern? Look at the AVID program for an example of one that is trying to do this.

7. Students have a lot of the answers and some good ideas about what makes a good teacher. What are some that have come up in this chapter? Why do you think we rarely ask students what makes a good teacher?

8. "We need teachers who be down for us no matter what." "They don't gotta be nice all the time, either. But we gotta know we can start over with them. Like our parents, I guess. Only they not our parents." Discuss these observations. What is this fine line they are describing?

9. College students once told me that they could tell who was in the best classes by the time they were in fourth grade: who would "make it," who would not. This is an example of institutional racism. What do you think creates this hierarchy so early? How can we change this? What will it take?

12

AFTER SCHOOL

Training Teachers

From the old phrase referring to a good deed, "That's white of you," to the New Age practice of visualizing oneself surrounded by white light, white has signified honor, purity, cleanliness and godliness in white western European and mainstream U.S. culture.

—Paul Kivel, *Uprooting Racism*

So I am divided. I want to be black, to know black, to luxuriate in whatever I might be calling blackness at any particular time—but to do so in order to come out the other side, to experience a humanity that is neither colorless nor reducible to color. Bach and James Brown. Sushi and fried catfish.

—Henri Louis Gates,
"Letter to My Daughters," *Colored People*

As I drive down Lyndale Avenue toward the freeway, I see Sheila with Ayana on her hip, walking toward the bus stop. Sheila waves, Ayana smiles. Sheila shifts Ayana to her other hip so she can reach into her pocket for change.

As I near the entrance to the freeway, I begin to prepare myself for my students at a nearby university. The class is "General Methods," officially entitled "Methods,

Media, Measurement." It is full of mostly white graduate students who have never taught. One young woman is Chinese American. They are getting their teaching license and their master's at the same time. They need this basic methods class for further advancement along a sequence of classes. Thus, they come from all fields of interest: Social Studies, Science, English, Phys. Ed. Because they have all been educated, they feel they are already experts on education. And they are—experts about their *own* experience in education, which often involves years at private schools, and sometimes no exposure to public education at all.

I park my car, stop at my mailbox to pick up revised class lists, grade sheets, and bulletins about meetings I cannot attend. I wave to a few of the adjuncts who have also arrived from their schools. They look as tired as I feel.

When I get to my classroom, most of my students are there, five minutes early. They do not smile or come up to talk with me. I have had other classes at this same university that have been delightful. This one is different. There are three young men who sit in one corner, baseball caps on backward, arms folded over their chests. They often feel it necessary to question everything either I or the visiting experts have to say.

It is not fair to characterize the entire class by these three. Yet, as do most teachers, I focus on the troubling elements in my teaching—the one hour out of five that doesn't go well, the one small group that misbehaves. I ignore the four hours that went smoothly, the students who are doing fine and, instead, mull over what went wrong, wake up in the middle of the night, anxious. The same is true here. I rarely think about the sweet women who ask perceptive questions or the enthusiastic young men who can't wait to get into a city classroom. I usually leave this class dissatisfied.

One of the young men, Matthew, of whom I am most wary, raises his hand as I begin the class.

"That last speaker on classroom management seemed kind of useless to me. I mean, I don't plan to teach in a school where there are going to be behavior problems like that."

"Where are you going to teach?" I ask. "The speaker was talking about problems in a wealthy suburb. Not inner city. They are everywhere."

"Small towns. They don't have that so much in small towns. It just didn't seem relevant to me." I know after three months with Matthew that he will never acknowledge my expertise or the expertise of the behavior specialist who had visited the class the previous week.

I have tried everything: powerful videos; provocative, informative readings; discussions; small group work; visiting experts. I am determined to
reach the three angry young men who sit before me, resentful, of what I cannot name. I am pleased that others—the young woman who thanks me for all
the articles and visitors, the older man who often stays afterward to talk about
the young people he works with at his job in corrections—seem to appreciate
the way I have been teaching. Yet it is the three men I cannot budge who pre-
occupy me, who throw me off.

It strikes me, suddenly, that these three students make me feel much more
hopeless and despairing about education and about our country than the young
men and women I work with all day at ASP.

OPENING UP MINDS

I walk around the room. I ask each student to choose two slips of paper from my
hand. I tell them they will have fifteen minutes to prepare a lesson for an interdisciplinary experience using the two disciplines they have drawn, no matter
how improbable: music and math, science and home economics, literature and
physics. They begin to work. When the time is up, they have some great ideas.
There is even some laughter.

Again, Matthew, the most outspoken of the fearsome threesome, says, "So,
what's the point? I'm never going to have to do a lesson with science and shop."

Susan, whom I like because she is enthusiastic, opinionated, and thoughtful,
says, "I think this opened my head up. I think I will look at the possibilities differently now." She is not trying to gain points from me. I know this. We have
talked of where she wants to teach. She is serious.

Next, I ask the class to look over an article I have provided for them on multicultural, interdisciplinary, inclusive education. While they read, I go and get
myself a can of juice. If Matthew continues to respond the way he has so far today, it will be a long three hours.

I want to tell Matthew exactly what I think. I want to say to him so many
things I will never say. I want to tell him I am weary of his voice and his arrogance
and the way he will not give me credit, for what I know with my body, what I
know so well from all the half-lit classroom mornings, in the hallways with tear-
ful and skinny girls. I want to tell him he is not qualified to judge our system

quite yet, be it in a small town, a suburb, or a city. I want to say that before he dictates what kids need from us or what we *should* be doing, he ought to experience the longings I experience. He ought to listen when one of my students comes to me with the news that she is going to have a baby, and she, the very same girl I catch some afternoons with her thumb in her mouth, is smiling for the first time with this news.

USING THE GIFTS OF
EXPERIENCED TEACHERS

These days, when *anyone* who has never been in a classroom as the teacher tells me that they know what it is like, I want to say to them, as I want to say to Matthew: "No, you don't." You don't know because you have not held kids in your arms whose cousins have died, whose uncles have AIDS. You have not tried to teach a boy to read who has marks all over his body from his stepfather's cigarette. You don't know what it is like to come home exhausted after battling the hard desks and rectangle forms of the bureaucracy for a child, just to get her some clothing for her baby. You have no idea what it is like to see truly gifted students passed over, disrespected, and let slide because of their skin color, their poor parents, or their addresses. You cannot even imagine what it might be like to see a brilliant math student be told to think about a junior college instead of the four-year liberal arts college where he could certainly excel.

I want to say to Matthew that in that small town where you want to teach, you will run into problems you cannot imagine now. I want to say to him that even in the private schools like the good Catholic one you went to, you may find unusual classes. Defiance may be the rule, and one young man or woman may take control in the blink of an eye, and you may be lost for awhile. I simply want Matthew and others to understand the gift of experience those of us who have been in classrooms for twenty to thirty years bring to him, to all who are new to this profession.

Such a diatribe would be unfair. I know that and so I do not say it, not in just this way. I coax, present data, show interviews. I want to bring these university students around to thinking about what they *don't know*, what they will learn from the students they will teach and also will learn from older teachers in the buildings where they will work.

HELPING NEW WHITE TEACHERS
CREATE INCLUSIVE CLASSROOMS

My students look up now, become restless. They have finished reading the article and are ready to talk. I open up the discussion, and they respond. Some of them say they are not concerned about multicultural education because they will not have very many students of color in the classes in the schools where they plan to teach. I ask them if they think this is the only time they would use literature or talk about issues and events involving people of color—in a school that is predominantly nonwhite. They think. They stop and think about it. They puzzle out loud.

I ask them to get into groups of four to devise a lesson for different types of classes. One should be for a class that is all-white, one for a class that is all students of color. Another one for a class that is half and half and a fourth for a class that has only one or two black students in it. The lesson is to be on any aspect of the United States' Civil War. What materials would they use? How would they present it? What could they use from science or even math to enhance a student's understanding of this war?

They go to work. I drift around from group to group. They are involved, engaged. When we finally reassemble and discuss our plans, I ask them to decide whether they would teach this lesson differently given the different composition of students of color in their classrooms. Most of the class members decide that they would handle discussion somewhat differently, trying not to make students of color feel they had to represent an entire racial or cultural group. They would ask students who are white to think about a white perspective on slavery. In certain basic ways, though, they feel they would teach all students many perspectives about slavery, no matter what kind of class they happened to be assigned, no matter its composition. I am pleased, as much by the thoughtful way they answer my questions as I am by their ideas. My nemesis, Matthew, is silent.

However, when the class is over he comes up to me. I am talking to a young woman who is planning to teach in St. Paul. I give her a few names of teachers she might contact in order to observe some classes. I am anxious to get back to ASP for parent conferences before I go home. As it is, Alan is there alone for the first part of the evening.

Matthew says, "What are you trying to get us to do in here?"

I am loading everything into my briefcase. My body language says clearly that I have to get going.

I begin to head toward the door. He follows me. "I want you to think, open your minds, question the way things were done and are being done."

"Why? We are just going to be put in schools that are traditional anyway."

I open the door to the parking lot. Matthew stays with me.

"Not everyone will teach in all-white private schools in small towns," I say.

"Maybe." He turns away. "You know this class really makes me angry." He turns back to me as I open my car door and slip inside. I open my window.

"Look. I would stay and talk, but I have to get to parent conference night at my school. Next week we can talk about your anger."

He turns aside without saying good-bye. He is less respectful than many of the young men I work with at ASP.

I head back out to the freeway toward school. I turn on the jazz station and am glad for saxophone. It is becoming twilight, seven o'clock.

I am amazed at how one student, be he in a public school classroom or a graduate course, can change the way the day goes. I remember one evening about a month ago when Matthew was not present. The conversation was lively. Students who had never spoken before, spoke that day, especially the women. When this young man is in class, they must not feel entirely safe. When he is gone, they do. It seems just slightly ironic to me that all the while I have been working to create safety for high school students, it is in this graduate class that I have not taken the effort to create a place where we can all feel free to talk.

I must have assumed that this class would be easier, that I would not have to work at creating safety. Why? Because it is almost all white middle class? Because these men and women are older, supposedly more mature? Well, I was wrong. I decide to call Matthew, talk to him directly. I have no idea how he will respond.

WHAT KIND OF TEACHERS DO WE REALLY NEED?

As I take a turn left at Marshall, head over the bridge and back down Lake Street to school, I remember a principal who said to me when I asked him if he thought we needed more teachers of color:

"Yes, we do. It is so good for all the kids to see role models up there in the front of the room: the white kids and the black kids, Native Americans and the Asian students. But we also need just plain good teachers. They can be white.

That's fine. I just want teachers who love kids and will work at it, who are not afraid to teach African-American studies, even though they are white and might make mistakes. The kids will teach them. They will make them into good teachers, no matter what race they are."

And then he mentioned that he often gets suburban middle-class African-American student teachers assigned to his school because it is primarily black.

"Funny thing is," he said, "these student teachers know less than a street-smart white teacher who has grown up in the city, about teaching the students here. Guess the university that puts them out here figures because they have black skin they can 'relate' to black kids right from the start. Some of 'em can. Some of 'em don't want to. I just want the good ones, be they black or white, to stay with me. Of course, I would like the best of all worlds, the street-smart, enthusiastic, good teacher of color . . . at least in greater numbers than I have them now."

TEACHING AS AN ART

When I think of my white friends who are fine teachers, who like and respect their students, and who include all their students in the curriculum in their classroom, I lose a little of the usual despair I often feel leaving my university course. Teaching, ultimately, is an art. It is sensing, each minute, each hour, what students are feeling, how they are reacting to the day, to the work, to the outside world. All I can do, as an educator of educators, is to challenge new teachers to be open to new information. I can encourage them to pay attention to the students' knowledge, to the fine literature, history, science, and even math materials and methods that are out there and that are evolving and changing each year.

And as for Matthew, I truly hope he does not go into teaching. Perhaps I can even advise him to consider something else as a career. He has gotten too much of my attention, though. For the last classes in this semester, I decide to focus on the others.

We need creative spirits in the schools today, whether they have been teaching two years or twenty. There is a place for brand-new teachers, full of enthusiasm and ideas. There is also a place for good veteran teachers of any race or culture, as mentors, as the wise ones in the building.

TEACHER TRAINING:
INSTITUTIONAL RESPONSIBILITY

I look up at the windows of my room. I can see the breeze blowing the curtains inward, a light on, and Alan's profile there. Our teacher-training institutions can play a large part in eliminating racism. They can do this through recruitment, of candidates for licensure, of instructors and professors for the university departments themselves. The more there are professors of color, the more young college students of color will see education as a place that welcomes them.

It is also up to these institutions to counsel those candidates who are not willing to learn and work with diverse students and curricula to get out of the field. I have been part of institutions that collect money, term after term, from students who clearly do not want to do the work of a public school teacher. These individuals will be passed along and will end up providing mediocre education for children in elementary and secondary classrooms around the country. I believe institutions of teacher training can be vigilant in their demands: for openness, for knowledge of subject matter, and for grasp of diversity and inclusive education. We must demand that students train in public schools if licensure is to be for teaching in such schools. We have often shirked these responsibilities and thus have perpetuated the problem of racist teachers and colorless curriculums.

In addition, when teachers' salaries are commensurate with salaries in other professions and when teachers' working conditions are reasonable, we may find more qualified applicants. When teachers are given the support they need in all areas, from clerical help to social services for students who are having problems, from small classes to a decent lunch hour, we might attract more gifted people to the profession. As more and more teachers retire, we have the chance to rethink this profession, redefine it, and recreate it in ways that make it a real choice for some of our brightest young adults, both white and of color.

REFLECTION QUESTIONS

1. What should we do about the Matthews who want to teach, who can pay the tuition, and who are resistant to all efforts to help them become open minded and receptive? Should they be counseled out of teacher certifica-

tion programs? Should there be separate licensure for private school teachers that would not necessarily license someone to teach in public schools? Would Matthew qualify?

2. As the proportion of students of color grows, not only in cities but in the suburbs, what are some unique situations that may come up for those students in the places where they are the only one, or perhaps one of two nonwhites, in a class? What do you think their situation would feel like and what can teachers to do address this?

3. Do you think open mindedness and flexibility, qualities that can make white teachers especially effective in urban, multicultured classrooms, can be taught? What would a course look like that teaches "relationship with students"?

4. If you set up an urban public school that provided optimum conditions for teachers, what would this school look like? Is it similar to elite private schools? In what ways is it alike and in what ways is it different?

5. What could the author have done to make her college classroom feel safer, given Matthew's behavior?

13

AT NIGHT

Community

The other issue is culture. If you don't respect the children's culture, you negate their very essence.

—Carrie Secret, *Rethinking Schools*

As I get out of the car, I am hit with a feeling of exhaustion. I want to go straight home. I want to curl up with food and television. Usually, we don't have many parents come in to conferences so I figure it will not be too long before I will be back with Maury and Max.

I walk around to the front of the building to enter. Nearby is an intersection that is changing. It is becoming a home to artists, a theater, new restaurants. While fast-food places predominate, there are a burgeoning number of coffee shops, Greek and Italian carry-outs, and small performance spaces full of smoke and surprisingly good food. Just a few blocks south there are still crack houses, drive-by shootings, run-down stucco buildings, and children out at all hours without supervision. Into these blocks come the long cars of white suburbanites making a buy, the beat-up trucks of long-haired kids handing money out the window, taking in drugs. There are also the black women on the pipe and gangsters strutting in fine clothes, dealing.

I live in one of the most segregated metro areas in America. Affluent whites often live in the suburbs, while the poor and African Americans, Native Americans, and new immigrants live in *certain parts* of the city. When parents of color come to conferences at regular schools across town, they often come into alien territory. Because we have an inadequate metro transportation system, they have to transfer twice, bringing their children with them on subzero nights. It is costly.

LANGUAGES FROM HOME

When I get to my room, Alan is there with Tyrone's uncle. Mr. Lewis has talked to me on the phone over the last year, and it is clear he is keeping an eye on Tyrone, although he has no financial resources to help out. He works two jobs at low pay and has three children and two grandchildren of his own.

Alan and he are laughing. Alan smiles at me as I put away my briefcase full of papers from my graduate students. It occurs to me that my students could learn more from one evening with Mr. Lewis than by doing three papers for me.

I can hear Mr. Lewis becoming formal as I enter: his tone and language change to "standard" English. A friend of mine, Rita, who is white and whose husband, Travis, is black, told me once that when Travis picks up the phone, she can tell if there is a black person on the other end or a white one, just by the way he speaks. He can shift within seconds, she says, between Ebonics and standard English. We do not often give our black students credit for being bilingual.

Mr. Lewis is pleased to hear about Tyrone and promises to come two weeks from tomorrow for coffee and cake to celebrate his nephew's graduation.

He pulls at the cover of one of Alan's books on the table.

"You going to college?" he asks.

"Metro State. I'm suggesting to Tyrone that he think about applying there, too."

"The boy ain't have any money, though," says Mr. Lewis, shaking his head.

"He might get a scholarship. With his test scores, he has a good chance."

"Yeah. I believe so. I believe you are right. He just needs to stay away from his brother. And that's not easy. Damon is a hard person to ignore."

"Ty said he was looking for a new apartment today."

"Hope he can find one. And he shouldn't tell Damon his address or phone."

"He has been able to stay out of trouble pretty well this year, hasn't he?"

"He be doin' it all himself, you know," Mr. Lewis says.

"I know. He is doing just fine," Alan says.

"Yes. That boy is going to make somethin' of himself. Of course, I can't tell exactly what that somethin' *is* at this moment, but we'll wait and see."

Mr. Lewis gets up slowly to leave, gulping down a few more swallows of coffee. "You tell Tyrone I was here, now," he says. Alan nods and walks him to the door. They go out of the room and down the hall, just as Josh comes in.

He sits down. I sit across from him.

"You know, Mr. Miller, Josh just needs to get to every one of his classes more often and he could graduate at the end of the summer."

Josh smiles. "That Josh," he says, shaking his head. "Just workin' at his job too hard, I guess."

"I don't think so. I think he is sleeping in, actually, maybe a little too much partying."

Josh looks aggrieved. "No way!" he yells, then slips back into role. "I think he is just putting in too many hours at his job. Although he does have this new girl-friend on the Southside. . . . " Josh pretends to muse, to wonder.

"So. Your mom coming in?" I ask, resuming my teacher role with him.

"No. She got to work the night shift. Just thought I would stop by, see how you doin'." He leans back in the chair.

"You get some lasagna?" I ask. As part of these conference nights, we have dinner for any parents and students who come.

"Yep. Not bad."

"Could you go get me a plate and bring it back here?" I ask.

"Sure, Landsman. Be right back." I look out my door as Josh leaves. I can see parents drift up and down the halls. Many of them are single; some have small children dragging on their hands, clutching at their skirts, their trousers. There are as many students here as parents. I have often wondered why our school isn't an evening school. I think it might attract more students, especially those who are trying to work day jobs and finish up their education. It might even attract some of their parents who have not finished high school yet or who want to learn computers. I have always wanted to teach in a real community school, open to parents as well as young people.

Alan comes back. He is eating ice cream. Josh comes in with a paper plate and some lasagna, a roll, and a carton of juice.

"Don't say I never did nothin' for ya, Landsman," he says.

"I would never say that, Josh. You just don't do enough for me in class."

"I know that's right," says Alan.

"Man, you two pick on me and I gotta get on outa here!" Josh tries to look picked on. He can't pull it off.

COMMUNITY:
WHAT WE LEARN FROM PARENTS

The three of us sit at my desk and work on the attendance charts. Josh helps out, reads me names, and counts days absent from my grade book. Alan fills in the wall charts to indicate what units students have completed, what is left to do. We do this for forty-five minutes or so, until Sheila's mother walks in the door. She is carrying Ayana on one hip.

"Just thought I would stop by. I'm takin' Ayana so Sheila can get herself some sleep. She's been real bad with the asthma right now."

"I know. She's been working hard, here, too."

Ayana is squirming and Ms. Parker puts her down. The little girl sits on the floor, clutching onto her grandmother's jeans. Ms. Parker is an attractive young woman, herself only thirty-eight. She is gradually coming around to helping out her daughter, by taking Ayana, by buying some medications that Sheila cannot get her medical plan to pay for. She was so angry when Sheila got pregnant that they were estranged for a year or so. Now they seem to be in contact at least once a week.

Ms. Parker sits down, reaches for the coffee pot, and pours some into a Styrofoam cup.

"That girl has got herself into trouble, though."

I am unsure of what Ms. Parker is referring to.

"I mean, she has got herself a bad news boyfriend."

"He doesn't go here, does he?" I ask. I have not seen Sheila with anyone in the halls and no one has stopped by my classroom to visit with her.

"No. He lives outside of the city. He's up to no good, I know that."

I am sorry to hear this. Ms. Parker can be hard on Sheila, but she can predict quite accurately what might happen with her daughter.

"Maybe she will break up with him. Maybe she will see he's not good for her."

"Long as I don't say nothing about him, she might!" Ms. Parker laughs. "The minute I tell her he is up to no good, she'll be at his place for sure."

We laugh together. We both know how stubborn Sheila can be.

I show Ms. Parker her daughter's chart, her progress in essay writing, and her application work for college.

"Oh, that girl is smart enough when it come to computers and reading. She's just got to get some smarts when it comes to boyfriends."

COMMUNITY:
THE NETWORK BEYOND SCHOOL DOORS

The light has faded to dark outside. Josh, Ms. Parker, Alan, and I sit together as the sounds below begin to fill the room: music from a car's speakers, and laughter from a bar with its door open across the street.

Josh gets up to leave. He smiles at me, nods to Alan, and walks out the door. He is an easy student, street-smart and calm. He is one of those urban white kids who might have a chance to make a difference, to build bridges. He is a natural at it, just as Tyrone is, and Sheila, too. While these young men and women may appear dysfunctional to a judgmental and academic world, I see in them a kind of possibility, a knowledge of race and culture, poverty and realism, that I rarely find in more protected kids.

It impresses me that Josh has shown up without any parent. There are always a certain number of students, white and black, Asian and Indian, who come on these nights without their parents. This can happen in middle schools as well as high schools. Adolescents actually like being with certain adults, even though they would never admit it to us. School is a place where they can talk, argue, debate, and test limits with us. I believe they like the structure we provide. But even more, they appreciate the personal connection teachers make with them, the relationship that forms over a school year, a semester.

Personal connection

Sarah comes in, dressed in white pants and a dark blue T-shirt. Her makeup is carefully applied and her hair is in soft waves around her face, shorter than it was a few hours before.

"Now you look ready to party," says Alan.

"You know that," she says. "I always party on Thursday nights. Reason I don't come to school on Fridays."

"Not a good pattern if you want to graduate soon," I say.

Ms. Parker nods her head. So does Alan.

"Well, I better just take my time graduatin' then." Sarah sits down and pulls out a can of Jolt.

"You'll be up all night on that stuff, girl," says Ms. Parker. She and Sarah must know each other. They seem familiar, as though they have passed some time together.

"Hey. I be fine. Sheila comin' to the party? That why you got Ayana?"

"No, girl. Sheila knows I don't baby-sit for wild party nights. She's sick with the asthma right now."

"Oh, yeah. She was lookin' sick today. Too bad." Sarah takes Ayana on her lap, puts her hands over Ayana's hands, and claps them together. The baby laughs, drools, and the wet line darkens on Sarah's white pants.

"Ooooh, girl, you got my pants all dirty! Now how am I going to find a nice place for the night you do that, huh, girl?" Sarah puts her face next to Ayana's, touching their cheeks together, breathing in the baby smell.

"If you need a place, you can crash at my house tonight. As long as you don't go to any party. Come on home with me." This offer comes from Ms. Parker.

"Thanks, but I'll find me a place."

The principal walks in. He shakes hands with Ms. Parker and says hello to Sarah.

"About five minutes. It will be nine o'clock. We're gonna close up."

Sarah gets up to leave, holds Ayana a moment longer, then sets her in Ms. Parker's lap.

"You take care, girl." This from Ms. Parker.

"I will. I always do, don't I? The Bridge has some extra beds. I can go there." Sarah smiles, a slightly uncertain smile. Again, just as with Josh, I am struck by Sarah's ability to interact with others in different communities. There is a kind of naturalness to it that is missing in so many places in this country. These students have much to give the world.

Ms. Parker gets up, heads for the door. Alan goes with her while I turn out the lights. As I turn them off, the outside becomes closer. The street lamps appear golden globes in an even row toward Uptown. I close the windows, hating to shut out that cooling air. Tomorrow it will be stuffy. Glad it is going to be Friday, though. I walk down the stairs, nodding to Jean Donohue, the Home Economics teacher from across the hall.

After parent conference nights, even when only a few relatives stop by, I am always impressed with the way students relax with us after school hours. It is good to be with them during a kind of limbo time, a time when I am not responsible for maintaining order, controlling the class. We need more opportunities for this in our schools, more ways to become part of our students' lives; time to learn from their parents, their uncles, aunts; time to feel a part of the community in some way.

REFLECTION QUESTIONS

1. What are some assumptions we make about people like the parents in this chapter? Why do we do this? How can we learn to rethink our gut reaction to a single mother, a father who is out of a job? Are our judgments and reactions complicated by race?

2. How often do we give credit to students, white and black, for the fact that they are more comfortable around issues of race than adults are? What does this mean for our educational training and emphasis? How can we reach this strength in students?

3. One of the ways to know students, parents, and communities better is to engage with them. What are ways we can do that? How could service learning projects work in this setting or in mainstream school settings? How do we do service learning without being condescending or imposing on the community we would like to work in for change?

4. Given the ways that schools are funded in this country, how can we change the inequities in education? When some schools have no media center, while others have two and computer labs and Olympic swimming pools, what does this mean about giving every child an equal chance to reach his or her potential? Can we do anything about this?

14

LIVING IN
DIFFERENT WORLDS

*I don't think black neighborhoods deteriorated because of the
departure of middle-class blacks. Middle-class blacks aren't different from the middle class of other groups. Doctors and
lawyers don't like to live like poor people. The only difference is
that black doctors and lawyers are stuck within a segregated
housing market.*

*It happened because stable working-class blacks became
poor blacks over the past fifteen years. The mobility wasn't so
much geographic as it was social and economic. They moved
down the income hierarchy from working class—or lower
middle class—to poverty status.*

—Douglas Massey, professor of sociology, University of
Chicago, as quoted in Studs Terkel's book, *Race*

When I am driving back down River Street, I lock my doors. I know black
people who talk about how insulting it is to see whites lock their doors in
a black part of town. They can see the knobs go down as they walk around a corner or from across a street. I also have black friends who tell me they keep their
doors locked in certain parts of town, too. There have been a number of night-
time carjackings on this stretch of River Street.

Katy and Jim, white friends, live in this neighborhood through which I drive each day. About one-third of those who live here are white. Some are Vietnamese, some Somali, and some African American. It is an unusually integrated part of this highly segregated city. One Saturday night Katy and Jim's son Trenton was picked up by police while walking down the street after his job, sweeping up and locking a nearby restaurant. He was cuffed, put in the back of a squad car, and driven to the scene of a burglary. There, in the back of the car, the woman who had seen the burglar in her kitchen, just before he jumped through a window, was told to look at Trenton. Then she was asked to tell the officers if he was the person whom she had seen leaving her house minutes before.

"That look like him," she said, "kinda Native American or Puerto Rican or somethin'."

Trent was taken to Juvenile Center, then allowed to call home. Even though Katy and Jim went to JC on Sunday with the owner of the restaurant, who vouched for Trenton's whereabouts at the exact time of the burglary, the officer in charge would not release him until Monday afternoon.

For six weeks, before his hearing in front of a judge, Trenton was put on "house arrest." Katy had to be with him if he left the house, except for the hours he was in school or at work. Katy had to give up considerable income from freelance work for these weeks. They paid a lawyer more than $1,500 to represent Trenton.

Finally, they arrived in court. The woman admitted she could not positively identify him as the person who had burglarized her home that night. She said that in the squad car, hands behind his back, with his dark hair and dark eyes, he looked like the man, but she could not at all be sure. Trenton was declared free and clear.

Katy and Jim were outraged. They went to a meeting of their community's block club. Most of the other people at the meeting were African American. Katy and Jim described Trent's treatment. By the end of their description they felt anger all over again.

As they sat down, they noticed smiles on the faces of the rest of the other men and women who had come together for this meeting. They saw them shaking their heads, nodding as they listened to the story, shrugging their shoulders as the silence fell for a moment.

"Happens to our kids all of the time," said one man. "My boy works at Mickey Dees and he gets stopped almost every week."

"Nothin' new to us," a woman says. "My Jerome was stopped yesterday evening after visiting his girlfriend. He was just walking home, and it was before curfew, too."

They were not unsympathetic, though, just seemed slightly amused at Katy and Jim's indignation.

I hold this memory in my mind many days. Tonight I hold it as I drive down the block, the same one where Trent was picked up. He has dark hair and eyes. Perhaps, this is what caused him to be stopped, perhaps no one else was around. And if Trent had reached for a wallet, if he had bad-mouthed the officers, if he had tried to run?

It is bad enough, as a white parent, to watch your sons or daughters disappear out the door to their jobs, team practice, tutoring, or rehearsals, wondering if they will arrive home safely. When our son lived at home, I remember the nights I waited up or tossed and turned in half-sleep until two in the morning when he did not call. Add on to everything the possible race-based reasons for his absence— that he might be in some jail somewhere, stopped for simply walking at night— and my life might have taken on a deeper level of anxiety, of expectation, of fear.

UNFAIR QUESTIONS

One of the most absurd questions I have ever heard is: "What do black people want for their kids, anyway?" Yet I hear this question all the time, from white graduate students, from people at parties where the subject of schools comes up, from well-meaning liberals at fundraisers for the latest political candidate.

It seems so hard for us to understand that a majority of black people want what a majority of white people want for their children: safety, hope, love, a good education, a future. Yet no one has ever asked me: "What do white people want for their kids?"

HOW DO WE COME TOGETHER?

I turn off River Street and onto 43rd Avenue. It is a quiet pocket of the city here, and as I approach my corner I can see a few people sitting on their front steps or out at the picnic tables in the small backyards that abut onto an alley. I can see televisions reflecting blue light from windows, an old woman in a house dress rocking in front of her screen. Someone is practicing piano in the house down the block. This is a quiet, mostly white, working- and middle-class neighborhood. It is not an integrated one and yet does not feel exclusive to me. Not like some of the more wealthy neighborhoods or some of the suburbs around Minneapolis that are fighting even the semblance of affordable housing.

Because of housing patterns, and high concentrations of people of color in the inner city, many well-meaning people see the only solution to integrating our schools and, ultimately, our society is to bus our city kids out to the sub-urbs. I am quite sure, however, that I would not want my son to be taken out to a school that does not want him. With all the talk of integrating with the suburbs, little is said about suburban young people venturing into city schools. It is usually a one-way proposition. While I have fought much of my life for integration, I find that now, these days, after much thought, I am com-ing down on the other side in this debate.

BRIDGES AND COMMUNITY SCHOOLS

I come down on the side of those who want to return to schools that are placed near their homes, that are easy to get to, that feel a part of the neigh-borhood that surrounds them. I say this with a great deal of sorrow and with some trepidation. Sorrow, because I worked in the civil rights movement to integrate institutions. Sorrow, because my simple dream is for us all to get along. Sorrow, because that dream is not now and may never be a reality, and it is the present that I am concerned about. Trepidation, because I am aware that if we return to community schools, we may find ourselves back where we started years ago, with unequal funding for schools in communities of color. Yet I believe that if we are vigilant about funding, perhaps even changing the formula for educational financing, and if we find parts of the week or even parts of each day to bring students from different communities together in our schools, I think we need to try community schools again.

We need to construct places of trust, where mothers can stop by at dawn to speak to a teacher before going to their jobs; where fathers can visit in the evenings on their way home from work.

Right now we build barriers to those of color who want to understand their children's school. We make them come from miles away. We array ourselves before them in our whiteness, rarely relieved by dark-skinned colleagues. We present all parents, white and those of color, with incomprehensible documents explaining their children's progress. We alienate parents constantly by our jargon, our inflexible conference hours, our unwillingness to learn about the communities from which our students come. To add to this, requiring them to come to our buildings from miles across the city seems unreasonable and an ineffective arrangement if we want to gain their trust and participation.

PARENTS EDUCATING TEACHERS

Too often, children in schools are rejected: for the way they speak, for the fact that their parents do not come to conferences, for the clothes they wear, for the way they learn. I believe that we reject students of color whenever we overcorrect our students who are enthusiastically trying to tell us a story in their language or dialect. I believe we reject them when we fail to include a discussion of black poets when we talk about famous "Southern writers" and when we make generalizations about black people or Asian people based on what we see in the media. It happens every hour in every city and suburb in this country. If we keep schools small, intimate, and part of the community the students come from, parents can check this out, stop such rejection more easily.

I love the description of a school in New York City called El Puente or the Bridge. The building that houses this school housed a community center *before* classrooms were ever installed, *before* the school was ever created. Thus, adults, old people, babies, and toddlers had always been a part of this building. When the school came, it came as part of the community, not as an intruder and not as a separate entity. It was organic, intimate with the center.

Unfortunately, our schools are almost opposite to this. They are stark, separate structures, isolated and surrounded by bare plots of ground, a few stores, unlighted parking lots. Perhaps we can begin to look for places where the community gathers and bring in our classrooms there. Perhaps we can build schools where we will be surrounded by small children, old people, or an occasional dog that runs in from the street. Perhaps we can create schools in places where cultures in the building, in the streets nearby, are integral to the very rooms where we teach, the holidays we celebrate.

BRINGING OUR SEPARATE
WORLDS TOGETHER: A COMPROMISE

Perhaps, as a friend suggests, we could have community elementary and middle schools, while setting up more integrated multicommunity high schools for our older students. If we create a sense of security and grounding in their neighborhoods when students are small, we could build places of common interest such as arts magnet schools, science programs, and other high interest sites they could attend as they get older. Thus, they would be moving further away from their own communities as they get ready to head to college, a job, or vocational school. There is no end to the creative ideas each city and each district could develop. And, if they are done right, these solutions would be as different as the people who make up the neighborhoods and streets, the barrios and the valleys of our country.

I turn in the driveway. The light is on in the kitchen, the dog is dancing in circles as I open the door. This is his way of greeting me. Maury's way is to call out from the television room.

"Hey. How was your fourteen-hour day?"

"Fine, except for the guy from my class at St. Thomas," I yell upstairs. I pour myself a bowl of cereal, add milk. I feel like a character from *Seinfeld* when I do this.

This is my refuge, from the other-ness of the world. I do what I have done for years. I detach from my day, watch some television with Maury, create boundaries so that I can sleep. I want to experience a psychic space between my home and my work world. I am better at this than I have been in the past.

A few hours later I turn off the light, lock the door, and climb into bed. I think briefly about the concert I want to go to on Saturday night. I have to order tickets. If I had the energy, I would get up and make myself a note. But I don't. Have the energy, that is. It is simply impossible to get out of bed.

Outside I can hear a baby cry from the house next door. Max curls in a spot of moon that comes in our windows. A motorcycle gathers speed at the end of the block, misses the stop sign near our house, and keeps going.

I drift off to city sounds.

REFLECTION QUESTIONS

1. What effect does racial profiling have on the every day life of people of color in our country? What might this be like, day after day, and what effect could it have on a sixteen-year-old boy who has seen this happen with his father, brothers, sisters, mother? Are whites and blacks truly living in separate worlds?

2. What do you see as the advantages to community schools versus busing for integration? What are the advantages to busing? There is not an easy, right/wrong answer, but rather this presents a decision many parents struggle with, especially parents of color who are considering sending their sons and daughters to primarily white schools where the resources may be better, but the reception of their child may be difficult.

3. What are some real, physical ways we can change schools to make students feel welcome?

4. Think of your own school experience. What would have made grade school easier for you? Middle school? High school? Given the prevalence of technology in the lives of our students how can we truly reconfigure schools so that we can take advantage not only of new sources of information but also of the strengths that students bring to us.

15

CELEBRATIONS
AT SCHOOL

*Why do we have such a hard time making school a happy place
for poor children and children of color? A few years ago, I asked
Oscar Kwageley, a friend, teacher, Yupik Eskimo, scientist,
and wise man, what the purpose of education is. His response
startled me and opened my eyes even more: he said, "The purpose of education is to learn to die satiated with life." That, I
believe is what we need to bring to our schools: experiences that
are so full of the wonder of life, so full of connectedness, so embedded in the context of our communities, so brilliant in the insights that we develop and the analyses that we devise, that all
of us, teachers and students alike, can learn to live lives that
leave us truly satisfied.*

experience

—Lisa Delpit, *Other People's Children*

TWO WEEKS LATER

Tyrone could walk at graduation ceremonies with North Community
High School. But then he would have to wait a few more weeks, and he
wants to feel the completion of it all, right now. This afternoon there is a gathering after school in the media center for the four students who are receiving
their diplomas from ASP. There are about fifteen others, all waiting to walk in

caps and gowns with their former schools. Many have already graduated earlier in the school year.

We stand around awkwardly. We hold cake and cups of punch. Parents sit on chairs, shake hands with the principal, congratulate their sons and daughters. It is subdued, no hats in the air, no practical jokes in the middle of the ceremony, no planes flying overhead as the speaker exhorts students to go forth . . . none of this.

"You going to look at Metro State?" I ask Tyrone.

"Yep. Gotta go see about registering."

"I'll go with you," says Alan, who is standing nearby.

Mr. Lewis comes in, looks around, and spots us. He reaches Tyrone, puts his arms around him in a bear hug. Tyrone tries not to smile but can't help it.

"You made it, man," says Fred Lewis. "You really done it, man!"

Preston comes in, bypasses the cake, shakes Tyrone's hand.

"I be followin' you man, right behind your back."

"I know. You only got a few more months." Tyrone is solemn.

Preston shrugs his shoulders. "I dunno, man. These tests are some tough shit."

"You just gotta concentrate when you get there."

The principal raises his hand.

"Just a few words and we will take some pictures for our collection," he says, smiling.

"I want to congratulate Tyrone, Mary, Martin, Tykesha. They have worked hard and have finished up some difficult years. We wish them Godspeed and good luck in the next years. We all know you will do good things out there."

We clap, lift our paper cups. Sam Bradley, a black man who teaches upstairs in vocational education, signals Tyrone, Mr. Lewis, and Tykesha that he is ready to go. Sam takes any African-American student who graduates out for a celebratory lunch. He has made this a tradition. All along, he reinforces these students for resisting the pressure: to quit, skip class. He even lets them borrow some of his treasured jazz tapes if they are interested.

Sam has pointed out to me that when kids listen to his jazz, they walk slowly down the hall, dreamy. He says we should give more kids jazz tapes, instead of all this hyped-up stuff they listen to now.

Today, Sam puts his arm around each of the young people he escorts out. Alan goes along, and Ty looks back at me. He stops, comes back, and puts out his hand,

"Thanks, Landsman."

"You are entirely welcome, Tyrone. I will get in touch with you about your writing. You should be getting it published."

He smiles again. This is the most I have seen him smile in months. It is over. He is on his way.

Fred Lewis comes back to me. "I want to thank you, too."

"You don't need to. You and Tyrone deserve the credit."

He smiles, turns to leave with Ty and Al.

The rest of the party drifts away. We teachers go back to our rooms to lock up.

I stop by the office to ask about the final days, room clean-up, who will be in my classroom for summer school, and what they will need.

No one says much. No "good-bye." No "have a good summer."

I walk out to the parking lot. Sam is driving away in his car, Tyrone next to him, Alan and Tykesha in the back seat. They are laughing. I wave. They all wave. I would have liked to have gone along. I ache to be part of their party.

I head home, playing old rock and roll all the way down River Street.

REFLECTION QUESTIONS

1. Read over the epigraph by Lisa Delpit at the beginning of this chapter. Look at the categories she includes in her thoughts after the quote from the scientist: "wonder of life," "connectedness," "community," "insights," and "analysis." Take each of these and consider how we could re-imagine schools, restructure and redo schools, to bring these elements into education.

2. "I ache to be part of their party." Can we accept that while we may never be considered part of certain communities, be they white or black or Latino, we can still work together, even love together? How do we form the bridges to those who are not like us, while at the same time not attempt to insinuate ourselves or assume a kind of acceptance that is not there? How does the power differential, the prominence still of whites in power, figure into this?

16

CELEBRATIONS
AT HOME

*Although it is fair to say that each and every member of Salt
and Pepper [a racially mixed choir] has been transformed by
the experience of performing with the choir, in important re-
spects we also remain the same people we were when we joined.
No one has changed color. No one has changed race. No one's
culture has been lost or sacrificed. We have managed to blend
and be respectful of difference at the same time. The only thing
we have given up is the right to dominate one another. No one's
history has been altered. But together we have the power to
transform the future.*

—Harlon Dalton, *Racial Healing:
Confronting the Fear between Blacks and Whites*

DAY BY DAY

Saturday. It is finally sunny on a weekend day and it seems that all my neighbors
are out in their gardens. Little ones toddle near the curb, are pulled back by their
mothers or fathers. Men and women stand with cups of coffee, talking about
where to put the impatiens, whether the snow-on-the-mountain is growing too
fast. I sit on my front step and watch Connor, the four-year-old from next door,
as he pulls his plastic lawn mower over the small patch of front yard in front of

his house. Across the street John Carlson comes out, waves before he gets in his car. He is dressed in his bus driver's uniform, on his way to do a double shift. Barbara, his wife, stands on the front stoop watching him leave.

On our corner, under the three fir trees, seven or eight young children play. They dig tunnels and line up their trucks, dolls, and little buses with figures bobbing in them over the rocky ground. They call this space the magic forest and have played here for years.

I can hear Bob cutting the lawn right next door. Joan, Connor's mother, Bob's wife, is forever and always with flowers when she is home. Her backyard becomes more pink, violet, and yellow each year. Now, she wipes her forehead as she digs up part of the front yard under her window boxes and lowers in tiny begonia plants, ferns, and, in the sunny spots, geraniums. Carol goes by in her white Volvo, already having taken Sam and Tommy to their Saturday swim lesson at the local Y.

It is Saturday in my neighborhood in the city and I don't move from this front step, not for awhile. I don't move because this is what I love most about my life, this quiet life on the street, this simple celebration.

On my block we are almost all white. I wish there were more families of color, wish there were brown-skinned children running the sidewalks. I am not sure why I want this or what it means about me. I only know that after five years of living in small Minnesota towns, when I arrived to teach at Phillips Junior High School in a largely Native-American section of our city and when I watched the kids going to class, I felt at home. I love to hear Ebonics. It sings to me, as the hesitant and unfamiliar rhythms of the Hmong students struggling with English sing to me, too; as the Latino/a and Native-American accents sing to me. I do not believe I am romanticizing anything here. I hope I am simply celebrating true and basic *differences* all around me.

I celebrate that this speech does not sound like my own. I also celebrate when Sheila memorizes Langston Hughes's poem "Theme for English B" and when she gets her baby the shots she needs to go to day care. These are the little day-to-day celebrations, of difference, of life steps, all in one week, or even in one day. They are what keep us going, almost subconsciously. Little Victories

NOT A QUICK FIX

So often, we mouth the words "celebrating diversity, celebrating our differ-ences," almost flippantly. It is easy to pay lip service to such words as *diversity, difference,* and *culture.* This is because we tend to stop on the surface of things. We want a quick solution, a tell-all session that will give us the secret and let us move on and get to the *real* business, whatever that is.

We are used to messages from the postmodern cacophony in which we live; these messages, commercials, and talk shows tell us there *are* easy solutions, there are recipes, pat answers, formulas that always work. Just as with finding the right carpet, discovering the right colors to wear that enhance your skin, or saying the right things to the man in your life, just like all these quick fixes, you, too, can learn to become "diverse."

This is not so. Celebrating difference can cause tension and complications for both white people and people of color. We are often bothered by difference, by a language we cannot understand, by a way of dressing that is not usual to us—a veil perhaps, or a yarmulke—a way of worshipping, a place of worship different from our own. And we do not talk about it because it may be tense, uncomfortable.

I was this way. For years I was afraid of friction, the separation, the mere fact of difference. I wanted a sameness, a kind of calm, smooth way of interacting with the world. I was brought up to want this. Yet eventually I realized that too much was hidden when I talked about race. I wanted to know what was behind a frown, a shrug, a "you don't get it."

Ever since college in 1966, when a man then called Stokely Carmichael (later Kwame Ture), of the Student Nonviolent Coordinating Committee or SNCC, came to a party in a house I lived in in Georgetown, I have wanted to know more about what those who do not live in white skin have to say. I remember that moment. He stood looking at us, drinking beer, listening to Bill O'Connell play the guitar, laughing. He said, "Oh! So this is what white people do at their parties!" I liked this comment, laughed along with everyone, black and white, who was sitting in the room. I liked the reversal, the flip side of all those comments I had heard about "those people" referring to African Americans.

Ever since my college friend Cheryl, who is African American, told me to stop using the word *colored,* I wanted to know more. Not that it felt comfortable being reprimanded by her, but it was even more uncomfortable not knowing what to say or how to speak.

Yet even though I have learned to welcome dissension, to argue with my father and to disagree with people in public, I still tend to become nervous when I feel conflict coming. I still want to smooth things over. I think many of us do, often at the expense of a real honest discussion about differences. I also believe we are getting better.

Our classrooms have a long way to go before we encompass a greater definition of celebrating diversity. We must allow for friction, edginess, dissension, and
discomfort in our rooms. At the same time, all of us, parents, colleagues, neighbors, and students, can find ways to celebrate our coming together in common
cause despite our differences and because of our similarities.

This last statement implies the acceptance of such differences, as well as the
acceptance of what we have in common. This is tough for those who want America to be a one-size-fits-all country. Such homogeneity is not going to happen. It
should not happen. Celebration of difference involves not trying to change others
to become like us, but rather taking pride in the fact we are not like each other.

We may or may not form true friendships with someone who is not from our
culture. Yet we can work side by side for affordable housing, integrated neighborhoods, a decent wage, and health-care provision in our school and our place
of employment.

WITHOUT COMPETITION

Here on the front step, I watch the kids on the block bringing water over to the
"magic forest," carefully so it will not spill. I see the group of them marking out
rooms for their shared "house," lining up pine cones for glasses, sticks for
knives, piles of needles for beds. I see emerge before me a whole living space, a
family, and a meal. They have all worked together. As they listen to each other,
the boys restlessly shifting from one foot to the other, the girls in charge, speaking with great authority, I wonder if it is naive of me to think this could last, this
spirit of coming together around a meal.

These kids, while not mixed by race, are mixed by class. Some of their parents work at lower-paying jobs, combining incomes that hardly allow them to
own or rent their homes; others come from families with much more. Later, they
may separate.

Or will they be separated? I am concerned that our schools do not depart
from the rest of society, from television and its images of women, from a government that denies assistance to all but the most destitute, from the movies that define blackness as guns and athletics, street life and gang banging.

Schools put children into categories early on.

Too many educational institutions are built on the idea of winners and
losers. We set up hierarchies early; the "top" students are the ones who are

headed for a great college, the "next best" will probably go to a local four-year university, and then maybe there are those who will go to a two-year community college, and so on, down the line.

Right now, in this morning scene today, such a hierarchy has not happened yet.

WHEN IT WORKS

This past year, on one of the days I did not teach at ASP, I was a visiting writer at a middle school. I told the students to choose two concrete details and one abstraction from a list I had before me. They chose "front porch step" and "a rose," along with the abstraction "justice." I said that often people use abstractions without making such abstract words come alive. I told them that a reader wants a sense of what an abstraction means in real, *touchable* terms. I asked them to try putting these three words altogether in one sentence, to make justice come alive with the details of a step and a rose.

Before they began working, one black girl stood up and asked me if she could "go out of the subject" for a minute.

I told her to go ahead.

She launched into a description of the way the brothers on her street, in her neighborhood, were always saying, "she fine."

"All the time they be sayin' this, you're fine, you're so fine." She looked at me and said, "But *fine* is an *abstraction,* right? What I want are some *concrete details* from these brothers, right?"

I asked her what details she wanted to hear, what *specificity* she would like from these young men.

"I want them to say things like, your hair sure do look fine with all those beads today. Or, you always be getting to school on time, you so good." She winked at me when she said this second example, making sure I knew it was for my benefit.

"You know stuff like that."

I responded that she understood the idea perfectly. She wanted details; she wanted specificity.

Later, at the end of class, she came up to me, her arm around her white friend.

"So we gonna go out and ask for *spec-i-fic-ity.* When those brothers say, 'You look fine!' we gonna say we want some *spec-i-fic-ity!*" she said, drawing out the syllables and smiling.

"Yeah, Landsman," said her friend, "and if we don't get it, we gonna come to you and have you go out there and teach those folks some *spec-if-ic-ity!*"

I laughed. They laughed. Their teacher, Native American, laughed. We celebrated.

This celebration is what I want for students in classrooms, their arms around each other. I want their own stories to become a part of math class, giving examples, asking questions from their neighborhood, their family. I want geography classes to talk about rivers: the Mississippi and fishing on Sundays, the passage from Cambodia, through Laos, on the rivers our students have crossed in the middle of the night.

I don't give up my white story for this. It is just placed side by side with the story of the young man who grew up in Chinatown and whose father is black, his mother Japanese American. It is there in all its New England beauty, on a par with the story of the girl who grew up in Chicago and whose parents are doctors and who is black.

We do not have to compete for the best story, the correct story. We can pass the salt and ask a question. We can serve the carrots and talk about math. I want our classrooms to be places where we do sit at the same tables, gather around, like the kids under the trees at the end of my block, figuring it out together.

I also want schools to be places where we celebrate that we are *not* color-blind: where we recognize the differences among ourselves in positive ways, in ways that teach us. I am wary of those teachers who declare they are color-blind. I want to ask them if they are truly blind. How can they not see the different shades of brown, red, and coffee color before them? I want to know why, to them, recognizing color is such a negative thing.

FINDING WHITE PEOPLE'S STORIES

When I taught Creative Writing at the State Arts High School, during an unusual year, it turned out that one-third of my class of twelve was not white. There was one Latina student, one Native-American student, one African-American student, and one student whose father had been born and brought up in Indonesia. When I asked the members of this class, all labeled "gifted," to write about family stories, myths, passed down to them from their ancestors, from their grandparents and great grandparents, the students of color in the class began to write furiously.

Tamika told about her relatives in Mississippi who talked about the ghost in her grandmother's house, where he came from and when he came out. She told a story of hearing him one night when she was little and that he was not frightening to her because she had been warned and she knew his story. Marie, the Native-American student, wrote about her aunts and uncles who lived on the reservation and the stories they told of winter nights, northern lights, and the ancestors who came back to sit by the fire and talk. Noah, the student whose father was from Indonesia, told about his relatives who lived overseas, what their house was like, what it was to hear their stories of fighting the Dutch, of the revolution, and of its cost. And Linda, the Latina student, wrote about family reunions, dancing, and color.

The white kids were all silent. They could not begin. Even after their classmates of color read their work, the white students in the class remained quiet, sad, lost, as though they had no stories of their own.

Because white people in this country seem so bent on being "individuals," I believe we have lost our connection to the communal aspects of our life. I know very little about my father's family or even about his childhood. There are a few family stories passed down but never a sense of coming from a people or a community of ancestors. I never heard about ghosts or felt a connection to those who had gone before me. That is why I believe that *to celebrate our place in the universe as part of a community of cultures is just as important for white students as it is for students who are African American, who are Asian American, who are Native or Latino/a.* It brings great joy to me these days to look at my ancestry. I feel a delight in simply knowing about the Guytons who were Huguenots and the Boies ancestors who escaped persecution for their Protestantism. I feel a part of some broader universe.

WITH CELEBRATION MUST COME HOPE

The neighborhood kids are all going home for lunch. I am beginning to feel guilty as Joan moves on to plant a new tree on the line between our two homes. I think I will go in to bake bread—something that will make me feel practical, a good homeowner, wife, baker, kitchen dweller. As I am leaving to go in, one of the boys going past me looks up and says, "Hey, Jules." I say, "Hey, Sam." He must have heard Maury call me Jules and tried it out himself. I like it. His eyes twinkle.

I know his parents have great hopes for him, for his happiness. I do, too. His privilege is shining here, and this privilege is hope.

When I think of the times I have lost all hope, of the times I have been clinically depressed, I know I could not imagine relief from pain—not the next day and not the next week. If any of our students feel this, for whatever reason, we have failed them. If they do not come to school, every one of them, with a sense of hope and celebration, each and every day when they arrive in our classrooms, we are failing them. We are failing all of them: the white boys in their thin sweaters and bare feet in mid-January, the black girls in veils and head coverings, the cheerleaders with their stick-thin bodies and their large, mascara'ed eyes.

If it is only kids who play on the basketball team or the football team who experience hope for their future, then we are failing. If the only times we celebrate as a school are during athletic contests and games, then we are failing. We are failing all those skinny boys in the back row of the bleachers who have nowhere else to go, all those girls who are good at charcoal drawing and have bodies that are round, and all those chubby black boys with glasses who want to be writers some day.

We must know that there are days when the students in our classrooms will close up—days when all the poetry in the world won't matter if the baby is in the hospital and they have chosen a little more food instead of a phone this month. At another time they will grab onto language. So we keep the language out there for them, every day.

What I want, then, as another way of celebration, is lunch in the classroom once in awhile. This is the metaphor I seek: an occasional alliance, a time of eating together, arguing a point, all of us relaxed and anxious or, as Toni Morrison says in *Jazz*, "welcoming and defensive at the same time."

I am looking for this to happen.

REFLECTION QUESTIONS

1. Think of some little day-to-day celebrations in your life. If you are a teacher, think of these in your teaching life as well as your personal life. Why do you think we so rarely give ourselves credit for these things, for

our accomplishments or the accomplishments of our friends and students? What do we want from our jobs, our communities? Are these different depending on our race?

2. What makes you uncomfortable talking about race or class or gender inequities? If you are white, what are your fears about this? If you are Latino or black or Native what keeps you quiet? Do you speak up when your support is needed in meetings, around kitchen tables?

3. How can we create true celebration in our classrooms and our lives? Why do we so instantly evolve into hierarchics, so quickly compete? Is there a way to encourage something other than competition among students?

4. One of the ways white students seem to have lost out in this country is that they seem to lack a sense of community and culture. Often they are encouraged to become remarkable individuals. Can we find ways to include both a cultural and communal and cooperative emphasis in our classrooms as well as support for the individual gifts each student brings? This is walking a fine line. How could we structure schools so this can be done?

RESISTANCE

The Power of White Activism

*But I also know that when there comes into being a critical mass
of people who, though they look white, have ceased to act white,
the white race will undergo fission, and the former whites will
be able to take part in building a new human community.*

—Noel Ignatiev and John Garvey, *Race Traitor*

Many friends of color are skeptical of those of us who are white and who talk of change and diversity. We have made mistakes over these years: have promised action and stayed with discussion. We have watched our own backs first and those of our colleagues or friends of color only after we have made sure we have gotten what we needed. Many of us have come to the table with the paternalistic idea of "helping the oppressed," of bringing our beneficence to the struggling masses of common folks. We have done this in the polite guise of community change, of foundation aid, of board membership, and we have done it imagining that we are bestowing great good on those incapable of getting it for themselves. We have come with condescension, false promise, and little follow-through. We have come with limited time to work things out, to disagree, or to argue. Rather, we often come in a hurry to bestow and get out, go home, head back to our own neighborhoods.

Yet despite all of this history, and despite my own daily mistakes, I still believe in the power of white activism. We can be antiracists at faculty meetings and at dinner parties, as well as in our classrooms and teacher lounges. I can seek out those in the communities where my students live—talk to parents, uncles, aunts, and grandparents and ask them what to do when one of the young men in my class disappears. I can begin to form alliances.

In alternative programs, when students are hungry or their boyfriends are after them, it is expedient to meet these students right where they are, *this* morning, *this* afternoon. And to meet students right where they are must involve an understanding of the racial history they have lived, as well as an understanding of our own racial history. It involves moving fast, to get a shelter bed, a college application, or even the right poem, the right story to read aloud to them.

I have learned so much over the years of teaching in such intense environments: learned by doing and failing and then being told how to start the next day to repair the damage. I have been told when I use words that might seem babyish and condescending. I have been told when I revealed too much by my facial expression: I learned how to keep a poker face. I have learned from those, many of color, who took me in, trained me, were honest with me.

FORMING ALLIANCES

Despite our differences, despite my association with power simply because of my white skin, I believe there are places and occasions when whites and those of color can come together. We do not need to live in each other's houses to form alliances. We do not need to break bread together every day or engage in confessional encounter group sessions to work for more jobs in the city. We do not even have to like each other to try and register more voters. And we can disagree. We can cry and fight and stomp out, and we can come back. We can break up alliances and reattach them again.

UNDERSTANDING ABSOLUTES

Once I knew a woman who claimed to be a pure relativist. She told me that Hitler was good, in a sense. He was good for some things: "Like killing Jews," she said. "Good for killing Jews." I remember that moment the way we remember moments that change us.

I stared past her and out the window to a woman waiting at a bus stop. She was black and her coat was thin, flapping in the cold March breeze. A small boy held her hand. I remember thinking that according to the logic of the colleague across from me, racists must be "good for" limiting civil rights or Klan members must be "good for" killing blacks. This conversation convinced me, more than ever, that there are some values that are not relative.

I have strong feelings about the goodness and evil that exist in the world. I believe that some things are absolutely true, absolutely good, or absolutely evil. There may not be a lot of these things. Most things have wavy lines, take on different colors in different contexts. Yet it seems clear to me that being the engineer of the systematic slaughter of millions of people is evil and is not "good for" anything.

I have an image I keep with me: it is of an eleven-year-old Hmong girl opening a closet door and seeing a wedding dress in just her size, hanging there. Suddenly, she knows that on the next weekend her parents will take her to the home of a forty-two-year-old man and she will be forced to be his bride.

If I can find her a place of safety, I will. If I can meet with her parents and with those in her community to talk about this custom, I will. However, I will not abandon my own conviction that it is wrong to force little girls to marry and to force them to have sex with men four times their age. I will fight for this girl and struggle with those in her community who insist on taking her to an older man's home. I will look to other Hmong women who are trying to change this child bride arrangement to be my allies.

My absolutes are in place and I know that sometimes they clash with the values of those in other cultures. Yet I can most often find women and men in those very cultures who will make alliances with me to work toward compassion for all children, girls and boys.

BRINGING ABOUT CHANGE
IN SMALL STEPS

It is in forming alliances and collaborations to fight for some of these few absolutes that I see some real hope. Compassion is a universal good. In our resistance to a lack of compassion is hope for change.

Paradoxically, it is often not in appealing to universals or abstract principles that change happens. Rather, change comes about in smaller contexts: in neighborhood block parties, when men and women come together to organize to keep drug dealers from dominating the corner. Change happens when black and white parents organize in their precinct to stop police harassment of young people. It happens in schools that are predominantly white when one isolated teacher challenges the racist assumptions of his administration. I have not abandoned a concern for national politics, yet right now I have little of the faith I had in the '60s that the government in Washington will ever support true, practical antiracist initiatives. I have abandoned trust in my national government to act with any generosity at all.

I vote and then shrug my shoulders and go ahead and look at what is happening close by. I look at my friend George, a teacher who organized students in his high school to silk-screen antigun posters to put in the windows of all the houses on their blocks. I look at the small press on whose board I serve and how it persists in publishing risky and important multiracial anthologies. It is with these groups and these people that I feel possibility for change.

WISELY USING THE
LIMITED TIME WE HAVE

I am thinking with more "specificity" these days. I am not spending as much time on abstractions as I used to. There are young people dying not too far from this neighborhood. The sauna at the end of my block is attracting more and more drug traffic. There are great poets in my classes who do not know they are poets at all. And Tyrone needs make sure he starts college and Sheila needs a phone *and* food. There is too much to do in the small sphere in which I operate for me to debate with "intellectuals," with "economists," or even "politicians" about the problems they see with affirmative action. I think we need affirmative action again. I don't want to debate this for hours on end, in a comfortable living room, in an upscale part of town, with people who should know better.

I like to laugh, relax, and eat well. But I don't do that when I am with racists. My appetite disappears at the first generalization, the first joke. I cannot sit and smile and lift my fork full of steak to my lips when someone says "if it wasn't for *those people,*" he would have a good chance at a job.

I also cannot stay in a room very long with parents of color who want to convince me that their sons, daughters, sisters, and brothers do not need an education. It is hard for me to respond to a parent who insists that her son be excused for skipping classes or should not have to do homework for me, simply because he is black, Latino/a, or Native American and I am white. With all its weaknesses, public education is still an important means of creating hope in children, in young men and women. And teachers, both white and black, can bring this hope home. We need cooperation in very basic ways to do this. We need help in making our schools safe, in instilling a healthy respect in all students, and in supporting our schools and our young people in reading, writing, and math. We need tutors and mentors, grandparents and parents, to advocate for their charges when necessary and insist on respect when necessary.

Right now I want to work with adults who want what I want: the greatest possibilities for our young people. I will join parents, students, and teachers, both of color and white, to resist classrooms that are boring and that provide only European curricula; to resist, as well, unwelcoming buildings, racist teachers, and poorly funded schools. I will join with those who want to get rid of institutional racism: gifted programs aimed at white students or the practice of tracking all students of color into Special Education.

I cannot raise my students. Sometimes it seems that I am being asked to do this and then criticized because I am not doing it perfectly. In classes of thirty to thirty-five students per hour, five hours per day, one teacher cannot possibly address all the needs her students bring to her classroom. In my subject, Language Arts, I can help to encourage students in what I know best: words, language, and story. I can teach them the "game of school" if those at home help me by acknowledging that it is important to know the rules.

We can resist together, Mr. Lewis and Tyrone and me. We can celebrate, too, Tyrone and me and Mr. Lewis.

REFLECTION QUESTIONS

1. What are some ways you can work in your community to bring about change? Who might be part of an alliance that could get a goal accomplished?
2. When you think about living a good life, what are some principles and values you cannot compromise? How does this put you in relation to other cultures and their beliefs?
3. What are some "specific" things you can focus on to achieve what you see needs to be done?

EPILOGUE

Max is whining at my feet as I put the bread in the oven for an hour or so. It is in simple round loaves, saltless Tuscan bread. The smell of it will soon drift out the window and into the street. Kids will stop for a moment in their careful construction of houses, castles, and caves and take a deep breath, wanting it. For now, I call up to Maury, tell him I am going to take Max out for a quick walk before the bread is done. Max twirls in circles when I pick up his chain, license, and leash. It is hard to get him to stop long enough for me to hook him up.

We start out. At the trestle there are no men in sight. We walk on by, easy and loose. As I reach the first bridge, I look back. I can see the turn-off to my house. Back there, Maury is stretched out on the couch, the bread is rising, and I am sure that Joan has started in on more landscaping.

Out here the river winds toward St. Paul, and from St. Paul it goes south to Louisiana. Once this river was full of fish, pure water. Once we did not live here, and only those with brown skin fished it. I know we cannot give it back. But perhaps we can make reparations of some kind. Because this history lives with us, just as the history of slavery lives with us, present, here, now. And so, too, the wild women and men are still with us, those who fought to free any people who were enslaved: black, brown, or white. Soon, I hope, we will celebrate what all this means. Soon we will mix our stories in ways we have never dreamed before.

Once in awhile, when we are teaching, our vision for the future is played out right before us. This happened for me on one day, in a third-grade classroom, in the spring a year ago. I had exactly the experience I am always seeking.

The class was made up of students who were black, Hmong, and white. The eight-year-olds and I were creating a "class character," a person the students agreed would be the protagonist in their stories. This character would be one they would discuss all year long. They would put him or her in different situations, creating narratives, and writing dialogues centered around this person and his or her life.

They called out ideas and I listed their suggested characteristics on the board. Gradually, our character emerged. It was to be a man. He was black, about thirty-five, a veteran of the Persian Gulf, now a veterinarian. He had "skin like chocolate," dark eyes, and curly hair.

"What shall we call him?" I asked.

"Charlie!" called out Demetrius, who was black.

"Charlie Boo," called out Lucy, who was white.

From the back of the room came another suggestion, but the student spoke so quietly I could not make it out. One boy next to her said, "She got a good idea. She say his name should be Charlie Boo Yang."

The entire class cheered. "Yea. That's it. Charlie Boo Yang."

"Okay," I said. "Anything else about him?" By now we had a pretty good picture of him: tall and black and a vet and a vegetarian (I figured they must be studying v-words that month) and his name was Charlie Boo Yang. He also had a dog and lived in a house in Portland, Oregon. He liked to play basketball when he was not working with animals. The students also decided that he wore jewelry around his neck and had a gold tooth in the front and was almost as big as a giant. I asked for anything more, any other details about his life we could decide on before we created scenarios with our new protagonist.

A white boy with freckles and red hair said, as the class became thoughtful, "I know!"

"Okay, Roderick. What else do you know about him?" I asked.

"He plays the harp!"

"Yeah," the kids said, their eyes delighted. "That's good, he plays the harp."

And there it was. That craziness I love when we let our kids play with words, images, ideas—all together as in this activity, or in solitude, dreaming, painting, reading about history, trying out different math equations. I love it when they come up with things I never would have considered, not with my logical, world-weary mind: like having Charlie Boo Yang play the harp.

It is not hard to find things to celebrate with the students in our classrooms. They bring these to us all the time.

REFLECTION QUESTIONS

1. What are some creative ways to get students motivated to participate? If you are a teacher or have a memory of an activity that worked in a class in which you were involved, what was this activity? Why do you think it was successful?

2. What is the reason the alternative school described in this book is still full of students of color? How do you think the public school system, education funding, and race or class prejudice might have played a part in this tracking? Can you give more examples of institutional racism like this? In the work world? The university world?

3. Finally, what is some good news you have heard or observed about the way we are changing in the United States in relation to racism? How can we continue to change for the better? How can we get comfortable making mistakes, dealing with anger, and admitting our own bias? What do you see, now, that you can celebrate? Who will you celebrate with?

4. Google "90-90-90 Schools" for a description of schools that are successful with students who live in poverty and are of color. How are these schools similar to, or different from, your own?

A FINAL NOTE
TO MY READERS

Dear teachers, friends of all colors and all cultures, who have read this book:

I believe that white people too often want solutions to be quick and easy. They want something they can follow and in a few months, a few years at the most, the problem will be solved. At the same time I believe people of color have known it will not happen this way. It will happen over decades, as our hearts change, our laws change, our responses soften, our minds open.

It will come when we have lived with each other side by side, when we have heard each other's stories. It will come as more children are raised in more families and schools where racism is challenged every time it happens, when the Tyrones and the Sheilas are expected to do the things white students are expected to do. It will happen when students do not belittle each other for trying to get an education, for learning standard English, for deciding to play the school game, the corporate game. It will happen when white and black students do not call others by the "n-word" or any other belittling language. It will happen when everyone thinks of everyone else as coming from a unique culture, respecting the strengths of that culture, studying the perspectives of all cultures in the curriculum, the history, the science, the life of our schools.

It will come when housing patterns change, when there are jobs at decent wages and health care is provided for all of us. It will happen when there is more economic equity, when greed is not condoned. It will happen when compassion and politics are no longer considered opposites.

We will achieve a day of freedom from racism when whites acknowledge the day-to-day privileges they and their children receive simply because of the color of their skin. We will achieve true equity in education for all young people, for all children in this country when poor, Asian, black, female, Native-American, and Latino/a students start at the same starting point as middle- and upper-class white children. When class sizes are small and when technology is up to date in every school in this nation, we will be on our way to equality. When all our children are well-fed, and when no one is subject to violence—when we are all safe, we will have reached a beginning to justice for young people growing up in this country.

In thinking about all these things, and in writing this book, I realized, finally, that we are each on our own journey of racial understanding. Mine began in a kitchen in Dallas, Texas, when a black woman told me not to use the n-word as I rhymed a rhyme, singing to my sister. It continued as I listened to my father use this same cruel word during my childhood. It has included laughter when Stokely watched us at a party thirty years ago, tears when I heard of Viola Liuzzo's death after marching into Montgomery with Martin Luther King, and hope when a Voting Rights bill was finally passed in Congress.

My life has been woven with moments of embarrassment at my own blunders, joy at my friendships, that high from teaching that comes at the end of a great day with students from all over the world, the country. I have been fortunate to have been in a profession where every day and every year students have challenged every stereotype and every generalization. I have learned all I know about race, culture, love, and celebration from them.

There is no end to this struggle. Across my street a family of African Canadians has moved in. Some on this very block were not happy to see Tolowa, Uju, Lesse, and Imecca arrive. A real estate agent showed Uju only houses on the Northside of Minneapolis, where many African Americans live, even though her work was at the university in our part of the city. I met her by chance and by chance we stopped at the house that was for sale by the owner, where she lives with her family now. This happened in 1999. Much has not changed, which makes it so important to maintain vigilance, to expect to confront racism at any time.

Other questions are theoretical and require more thought. My nephew has married a young white woman from South Africa, who moved here with her family when she was four years old. Is she African American?

What does it mean that young Somali men want to make it clear they are not native-born black Americans because they do not want to be treated so badly?

It is because these kinds of questions never stop being asked, that this reflection never ends. They challenge the assumptions embedded in the language, our theories, our definitions of "race" itself. It is because of such questions that the conversations expand and open up. As a teacher and as a white person, I feel privileged in more ways than skin color to have known the white and black activists, writers, artists, mothers, fathers, kids, and friends who have been patient with me all along the way. This book is a way of thanking them for their good and compassionate instruction over these fifty-six years of my life.

GOOD NEWS

As I was finishing this book, I was invited to come back to the alternative school where I had spent the year documented here. It has changed in so many good ways: the counselors are working hard to get young men and women thinking about college; the teachers are providing creative, exciting classes with lots of discussion and outside artists; and the new administrators and front office staff are welcoming yet firm. There has been a necessary turnover, as teachers who did not want to be there retired and others transferred. Most important of all, the teachers who now teach there are a dynamic group of men and women who like working with their students. It is an exciting place to be in many ways. Attendance is still not consistent enough, and the students still come with the same kind of serious life crises and problems as the year I was at ASP.

Also, and most relevant to this book, the students still look to be primarily black and Latino/a, Native American, Hmong, and now Somali. They are the students we fail to reach in our regular schools, in our Social Services networks, and on the streets. They are often poor and have been in trouble with the courts. Some are homeless. Their numbers reflect the failure of this country to come to terms with its innate and soul-deep racism. While I am pleased to see ASP such a vibrant place, with caring and firm teachers and administrator, I am still too aware of the color divide in our country when I visit. I am still concerned about what we have done and have not done as a nation to perpetuate such a divide. All I am left with is the importance of speaking about these things and bringing my words to bear.

REFERENCES

Ayers, Bill. "Racing in America." In *Off White Readings on Race Power and Society*, ed. Michelle Fine, Lois Weis, Linda C. Powell, and L. Mun Wong. New York: Routledge, 1997.

Baldwin, James. "Many Thousands Gone." In *Notes of a Native Son*. Boston: Beacon Press, 1955.

———. "Stranger in the Village." In *Notes of a Native Son*. Boston: Beacon Press, 1955.

Banks, James. "Approaches to Multicultural Curriculum Reform." *Multicultural Leader* 1, no. 27 (Spring 1988).

Bryant, Philip. *Sermon on a Perfect Spring Day*. Minneapolis, Minn.: New Rivers Press, 1998.

Dalton, Harlon L. *Racial Healing: Confronting the Fear between Blacks and Whites*. New York: Anchor Books Doubleday, 1995.

Delpit, Lisa. *Other People's Children*. New York: The New Press, 1995.

Du Bois, W. E. B. *Souls of Black Folk*. New York: Bantam Books, 1903.

Gates, Henry Louis, Jr. "Letter to My Daughters." In *Race: An Anthology in the First Person*, ed. Bart Schneider. New York: Three Rivers Press, 1997.

Haynes, David. *Right by My Side*. Minneapolis: New Rivers Press, 1993.

Ignatiev, Noel, and John Garvey, eds. *Race Traitor*. New York: Routledge, 1996.

Kivel, Paul. *Uprooting Racism: How White People Can Work for Racial Justice*. Gabriola Island, British Columbia, Canada: New Society Publishers, 1996.

Moyers, Bill. *The Language of Life*. New York: Doubleday, 1995.

Obama, Barack. *Dreams from My Father*. New York: Kodansha International, 1996.

Roethke, Theodore. "The Waking." In *The Complete Poems of Theodore Roethke*. New York: Anchor Books, 1966.

Secret, Carrie. "Embracing Ebonics and Teaching Standard English (Milwaukee, Wisconsin)." *Rethinking Schools* 12, no. 1 (Fall 1997).

Simon, David, and Edward Burns. *The Corner.* New York: Broadway Books, 1997.

Tatum, Beverly. *Why Are All the Black Kids Sitting Together in the Cafeteria?* New York: Basic Books, 1997.

Terkel, Studs. *Race.* New York: Doubleday Anchor, 1992.

Walker, Alice. *Anything We Love Can Be Saved.* New York: Random House, 1997.

ACKNOWLEDGMENTS

In addition to all the students I have worked with over twenty-five years of teaching in public schools, I would like to give great thanks to the following colleagues and friends who have been responsible for bringing this book into existence:

to Jehanne Beaton for her careful reading of the manuscript-in-progress and her support over the years;

to Linda Norlander and Marcia Peck for their original thoughts on my first draft and their constant encouragement;

to Mary Easter for her constant encouragement, support, and the joy she brings over our lunches together;

to Bill Ayers, Sue O'Halloran, David Haynes, Jill Breckinridge, Leni Roulis, Carey Clark, Anita Beaton, John King, Tom Kitto, and George Roberts, for their deep friendship and insight into the subject of race and culture;

to Deborah Appleman for her constant encouragement and belief in my work;

to Ruth Katz for her many phone calls and a willingness to listen always;

to Catherine Furnberg for the personal insights she inspires in me that allow me to go on talking and making mistakes and coming back again;

to Peggy McIntosh for her suggestions, responses, and support and help in the drafts of this book, and for her original and inspiring work on white privilege;

to the Minnesota Inclusiveness Program for their great and patient training sessions for S.E.E.D. seminar leaders (Seeking Educational Equity and Diversity);

to Lisa Delpit for enlightening me with her important work;

to Natalie Goldberg for her encouragement and enthusiasm for my work always;

to the Norcroft retreat and Joan Drury for providing a place to think about this book;

to students in the Hamline Learning Community for their willingness to speak from their hearts;

to the many teachers I have worked with and taught, both white and of color, who have taught me so much about what it means to celebrate students' accomplishments everywhere;

and, as always, my love and affection to Aaron, my son; his wife, Johanna; and my husband, Maury, for providing me with the center that allows me to go out into a complicated world.

The author and publisher gratefully acknowledge permission to use quotations from the following sources:

Notes of a Native Son, by James Baldwin. Copyright © 1955, renewed 1983, by James Baldwin. Reprinted by permission of Beacon Press, Boston.

"Ottawa, MN, Cemetery—1992 In Memory of Otto Spavek," from *Sermon on a Perfect Spring Day* by Philip Bryant (Minneapolis: New Rivers Press, 1998). Reprinted by permission of the author.

Racial Healing: Confronting the Fear between Blacks and Whites, by Harlon L. Dalton (New York: Anchor Books Doubleday, 1995). Reprinted by permission of the publisher.

Other People's Children: Cultural Conflict in the Classroom, by Lisa D. Delpit. Copyright © 1995 by Lisa Delpit. Reprinted by permission of The New Press.

The Souls of Black Folks, by W. E. B. DuBois (New York: Bantam Books, 1903).

Colored People, by Henry Louis Gates (New York: Knopf, 1994). Reprinted by permission of the publisher.

Race Traitor, edited by Noel Ignatiev and John Garvey (New York: Routledge, 1996). Reprinted by permission of the author.

Uprooting Racism: How White People Can Work for Racial Justice, by Paul Kivel (Gabriola Island, B.C., Canada: New Society Publishers, 1996). Reprinted by permission of the publisher.

"The Waking," by Theodore Roethke, from *The Complete Poems of Theodore Roethke* (New York: Anchor Books, 1966). Reprinted by permission of the publisher.

ACKNOWLEDGMENTS

"Embracing Ebonics and Teaching Standard English," interview with Carrie Secret from *Rethinking Schools* 12, no. 1 (Fall 1997). Reprinted by permission of *Rethinking Schools*.

The Corner: A Year in the Life of an Inner City Neighborhood, by David Simon and Edward Burns (New York: Broadway Books, 1997). Reprinted by permission of the publisher.

The Language of Life, by Bill Moyers (New York: Doubleday, 1995). Reprinted by permission of the publisher.

Why Are All the Black Kids Sitting Together in the Cafeteria? by Beverly Daniel Tatum. Copyright © 1997 by Beverly Daniel Tatum. Reprinted by permission of Basic Books, a member of Perseus Books, L.L.C.

Anything We Love Can Be Saved, by Alice Walker (New York: Random House, 1997). Reprinted by permission of the publisher.

APPENDIX A

Strategies for Meeting the Needs of Economically Struggling Students

1. Assume all students can learn and can learn complicated and creative material.
2. Build a classroom and a school that gives control to students as much as possible while at the same time maintaining safety and structure. Allow their voices and interests to drive your curriculum.
3. Check on your own assumptions about poor kids or their parents: Do not assume they are not as smart as other kids, that they do not want to learn, that they cannot learn in creative and unusual ways. Do not assume they all learn in one way or must be taught in a rote method, at the expense of teaching them ways of thinking critically, writing creatively, or learning the scientific method, the Pythagorean Theorem.
4. Think of the assets students who live in poverty bring to the classroom, not always the deficits. Resiliency, perseverance, flexibility, compassion, and even hope are just a few of the things some of these kids and their parents have learned.
5. Do not believe in stereotypes about poor students or generalize about them. Use information and data to understand situations, yet be careful of assuming behaviors or states of mind for any whole group. This comes dangerously close to stereotyping.
6. Become reflective and self-reflective about why kids are without so much in our cities and neighborhoods. Don't be afraid to question the assumptions of others about these kids and their families. Be willing to speak up

when destructive or negative comments are made about any whole group. Avoid the poison of the teacher's lounge if that is the way it is in your school.

7. Ask yourself: What do I control? Who are my allies? And go from there. Understand you cannot change the world, but can work within your classroom and community to create change. Be willing to really look at what you control: the building itself, the curriculum, the presence or absence of music as part of your curriculum.

8. Support teachers and colleagues who are challenging students and who are finding ways to reach them. Build a support network for those teachers in your building. Find ways for them to connect even if it is once a week by email, or in the media center talking about "what went right this week" each Friday. Be imaginative about this support.

9. Remember, deciding on what to do in schools does not mean making the decision between treating kids like human beings versus academic and skill achievement.

10. Keep your own boundaries clear when working with students in trouble or who are in need of so much. Maintain your "other life" so that you can go into the classroom whole heartedly, ready to meet kids with your heart and mind and without resentment. This is what they need from you the most.

11. Expand the notion of school functions: Can schools provide evening support groups for parents? Can they develop evening classes for both students who need credits and parents who also want to learn or get high school credit? Can they provide child care for parents who want to come to conferences, transport parents to meetings, or even hold conferences in another building? Can teachers visit the neighborhoods from which their students come? The list here is endless.

12. Find ways to provide the basic necessities: a place to wash clothes; a drive for coats for the winter for students; breakfast, snack, and lunch programs; funding from businesses for supplies, computers, keyboards, art materials.

13. Do not assume all kids have: computers; phones; a regular place to live; access to pencils, books, supplies; enough food; a place to wash clothes; a feeling of safety when they go home; a place to fall asleep when they are tired.

14. Look in the community for resources for kids: small churches that can provide a place to do homework, a community leader the kids respect, a shop where kids parents' go to talk and hang out.
15. Find a way to survey students at the beginning of the year or your class time with them. In this way you will learn a lot about their home situation.
16. Ask students to do jobs for you, making them feel important and also in control of something in their lives.
17. Do not single kids out or even indicate in front of others that you know they are homeless or poor, yet make yourself available for them to come in and talk with you. Refer them for help when this happens.
18. While you do not want to coddle students, you may also "cut deals" with some of them. If they do not bring their homework in some day because they have been out at night trying to find a place to sleep, figure out a time to help them get the homework done in school. Thus you are not letting them get away with not doing it at all, but you are making a deal with them about how to get it done.
19. Convince students, in whatever capacity you hold in a building, "I mean business, I believe you can learn, and I will listen to you, giving you meaningful work to do." Provide them with a way to work at their level to achieve a grade, helping them increase skills without frustrating them. Make assignments open-ended.
20. Counsel out teachers who do not believe all students can learn.

APPENDIX B

Classroom and Building Assessment: High Expectations

_____ Materials and examples include works, ideas, concepts by a diverse group of authors, thinkers, historical figures, and so on.

_____ Diverse groups are woven in, not separated out of overall curriculum.

_____ Texts, content, issues, and so forth, are chosen with knowledge of what issues can come up, with thought beforehand about how to provide a place for a safe discussion.

_____ All students are made to feel safe in the classroom, hallways, lunchroom, and so on.

_____ Generalizations about racial and ethnic groups are simply not part of the vocabulary of the school by anyone.

_____ Evidence of many cultures can be seen on walls, in the library, in adults in the building, in examples used in classrooms, in literature, celebrations, and so forth.

_____ Students' and parents' discomfort, frustration, anger, are taken seriously and ways of mediation and discussion are provided to work things out.

_____ High expectations are provided for all students: to get work in, to complete work, to know the answers to different levels of questions, to work in class, to follow class guidelines, to respond to parent calls, to respond to structure.

_____ Parents of color are present and feel welcome at conferences, celebrations, dinners, and are part of parent councils, parent advisory groups.

_____ Students of all ethnicities are in all levels of learning in a building, that is, there are no "all white" or "all students of color" tracks, programs, and so on.

_____ Students of color are counseled to consider college, academic programs.

_____ Administration and teachers are willing to counter racist comments and low expectations of students of color in lounges, meetings, individual discussions, committee meetings.

_____ Teachers are aware of the importance of inclusive curriculum and education even when schools are primarily white: a matter of telling the complete truth.

_____ Teachers and staff are comfortable discussing issues of race, class, and gender without being defensive or being shamed.

_____ Teachers and staff are willing to go do the hard work of dealing with racism in the building and are willing to change when it is necessary.

_____ Teachers and staff are confident in their ability to talk about and deal with issues of race and inclusiveness, aware that they are always in flux and will learn new things each day that may make them uncomfortable.

_____ Teachers are willing to reach out intellectually, meet face to face, and step out and into another environment to work toward activism and enlightenment.

ABOUT THE AUTHOR

Julie Landsman taught in the Minneapolis Public Schools for twenty-five years. The students she taught have been called learning-disabled, high-risk, troubled, mainstream, gifted and non-English speaking. She is not fond of labels and prefers to call them by their names: Tanya, Mai, Jamal, and Susan, to list just a few. Landsman has taught at St. Thomas and Hamline Universities, and she has consulted with teacher training programs at the University of Minnesota, Carleton College, Macalaster College, and other colleges in Minnesota. She also taught creative writing for three years at the Minnesota State School for the Arts.

Landsman retired from public schools and is now teaching at Hamline University, training teachers in Minneapolis schools, and working on her third book, *Living with Men.* Her first book—*Basic Needs: A Year with Street Kids in a City School,* a memoir published by Milkweed Editions—won a Minnesota Book Award in 1994. Her book *Tips for Creating a Manageable Classroom* was published in 1994 by Milkweed. Landsman has edited two anthologies: *From Darkness to Light: Teens Write about How They Triumphed over Trouble* (Fairview Press, 1995) and, with David Haynes, *Welcome to Your Life: Writings for the Heart of Young America* (Milkweed Editions, 1999). Her poetry, articles, and memoirs have been published in small and large press publications, and Landsman has received grants and awards for her writing, including a travel writing grant from the Jerome Foundation.

Landsman lives in Minneapolis with her husband, Maury, and her dog.

Curriculum - (27), 184, 45, 30, 57, 36, 37, 183, 40
(173), (187), 51, 80, 34, 29, 56, 168

Intersection - 12

Double con - 70